LIVING LONGER AND LOVING IT

Deborah Geller
and
Arthur Geller

HAMMOND INCORPORATED
MAPLEWOOD, NEW JERSEY

Library of Congress Cataloging in Publication Data
Geller, Arthur.
  Living longer and loving it.
    1. Aged—United States—Biography. 2. Aged—United States—Attitudes. I. Geller, Deborah, joint author. II. Title.
HQ1064.U6G35   301.43′5′0973   78-5851
ISBN 0-8437-3409-4

ENTIRE CONTENTS COPYRIGHT © MCMLXXIX BY HAMMOND INCORPORATED
All rights reserved. No part of this book may be reproduced or utilized in any form or by any means, electronic or mechanical, including photocopying, recording or by any information storage and retrieval system, without permission in writing from the publisher.
PRINTED IN THE UNITED STATES OF AMERICA

To both our mothers:
Ida Geller and Annette Goodfriend

Contents

The Reasons vi

Acknowledgments viii

Introducing a Brighter Shade of Gray 1
  Ollie Randall 11
  Nelson Cruikshank 16
  Maggie Kuhn 25

A Time for Doing 31
  Tom McKenna 34
  Ed Rawson 38
  Ethel Rucks 43
  James MacKay 46

Still on the Job 51
  Herman Langsner 55
  Todd Duncan 58
  Walter Stack 61
  Ruth McFadden 65
  Vera Lachman 69

Back to School 73
  Charles Niles 77
  Solomon Novick 81
  Richard Newson 86

Gray Power 90
  Jean Hopper 94
  Francis Brown 99
  Jack White 103
  Alice Van Landingham 106
  Ruth Haefner 111

Life at the Center 115
  William Doughaday 119
  James Markham 123
  Frieda Sousa 127

For Art's Sake 133
  Howard Hanson 137
  Joseph Konzal 141
  Ruth Bernhard 144
  Peter Blume 149

Taking a Chance on Love Again 155
  Malvina and John Brown 159
  Mary and Fred Taylor 164
  Bea and John Morrow 168
  May and George Brookman 173
  Madeline and Walter Baer 178

The Reasons

Americans appreciate underdogs and root for those with limited resources who are willing to struggle against great odds in order to realize their dreams. And should the underdog win, we thrill to his success. Inspired by their example, we frequently attempt something bolder than usual in our own lives. Believing that older persons are underdogs in American society, the writers thought that potential readers, both young and old, would respond to an upbeat book about the elderly in America with an enthusiasm that could favorably affect the situations of both those who are old now and those who one day will be among the elderly.

There is not exactly a dearth of books on the subject of aging. However, most of them have been written by specialists in the field for other specialists, employing language that is usually too abstract or technical for the general reader. There is also a tendency to emphasize the gloomiest aspects of aging, which has contributed to a number of misconceptions.

Without denying the problems, we felt that it would be possible to show the reader how elderly people manage to overcome the odds. Further, we decided that the best way to present such a book would be to have some representative older persons tell their stories in their own words. This approach would hopefully result in a book whose firsthand voice would be personal, immediate in feeling, very real, and accessible to the general reader. We interviewed older people from different sections of the country and from different socio-economic groups to demonstrate that, despite differences, there was a basic commonality of experience. Some were referred by friends, but most were contacted for us by friendly colleagues in the field of aging.

Another strategy was to select people who were achieving their goals in different ways, so that we could offer the reader a better understanding of various issues which strongly engage the elderly. For the most part, we selected people who are not now, nor ever have been, famous. We wanted to show that courage, determination, love, vitality and resourcefulness — virtues that one can only admire — do not belong solely to prominent persons. They are qualities also possessed by those elderly whose lives have received little attention.

A few words about the interviews, which were conducted from the spring through the winter of 1977. The passage of time and events since then may make some comments seem dated. However, for obvious ethical reasons, we did not want to alter the interviews, and so did not change words to fit facts. Likewise the ages of those interviewed remain in the book as they were when presented to us in 1977. For practical reasons, mainly the authors' job responsibilities, only a few of the interviews were done face-to-face. All the others were taped over the telephone. After some lengthy discussion as to whether this technique could work, we concluded that it might be an advantage. We thought that it would relax, rather than alienate the interviewees, and they would be more responsive to a friendly telephone voice than to an interviewer confronting them in person. It's difficult to determine whether or not our judgment was accurate. However, on several occasions the interviewees said that they could speak candidly because they were talking to a telephone. It was probably helpful for some and for others unimportant.

For both authors, the interviews were an unusual and special experience. During these lengthy, highly personal conversations, we moved rapidly from the sense that we were strangers getting acquainted to a feeling of having become friends with people whom we would want as friends, listening as they talked about their life experiences in an interesting, lively and sensitive manner. The interviews invariably ended with mutual invitations to get together should either of us be in the others' hometown. We were also very reluctant to end an interview. It was as though we were saying goodbye to a close friend with whom the next meeting was uncertain.

We hope that the reader will have similar feelings of affection and pleasure meeting the older people within our book.

ACKNOWLEDGMENTS

First, our profound thanks to those older persons who consented to share their life experiences with us and so made this book possible. We are also very appreciative of the efforts made by our friends in the Delegate Council of the National Institute of Senior Centers, who contacted and recommended us to most of those we interviewed. They are: Sol Boskind, Lucille Costello, Inez Edwards, Freida Gurrecht, Ann Johnson, John Paul Jourard, Richard Halvorson, Shirley Overland, Pat Taylor, Ann Truit and Leon Wolf. It would be impossible to list all the individuals who helped us obtain the facts and figures that we needed, so a collective thanks to the various staffs at: U.S. Census Bureau; Region II office of the Administration on Aging; U.S. Department of Health, Education, and Welfare; Gray Panthers; American Association of Retired Persons; National Council on Aging; National Council of Senior Citizens; Research Department of the New York City Department for Aging.

Our thanks to Pamelia Perkins for her editorial assistance. We are also grateful to Frank Brady, friend and editor, who suggested that we write a book about the positive aspects of aging. And to Dorothy Bacheller, copy editor at Hammond, our enormous gratitude for her patience and skills in bringing order to chaos on several occasions.

We would like to acknowledge that a portion of the interview with Maggie Kuhn was quoted with permission from the WNET—New York interview with Maggie Kuhn, "A Wrinkled Radical," copyright 1975 by Educational Broadcast Corporation.

Introducing a Brighter Shade of Gray

What is old and who is old are questions that every society answers in many complex, subtle and different ways, so that usually everyone knows the answers without having to ask too many questions. Whether or not one likes the answer is, of course, another question. Here in America, the age of sixty-five has come to mean old, primarily because it has been until recently the age of retirement and when most people begin to receive their Social Security benefits. Interestingly, in Sweden the retirement age is seventy, while in India it's fifty-five. The concept of old varies from place to place, depending pretty much on the life expectancy of its people. But sooner or later, we will all be old, no matter where we live, if we live long enough.

The briefest glance at a few demographic charts reveals that America's almost legal definition of what is elderly now includes more older persons than at any time in our history. According to present trends, the number will continue to multiply significantly until around 2020. At the beginning of this century there were slightly more than three million men and women aged sixty-five and over, just four percent of the population. Today there are more than twenty-three million people in that age bracket, over eleven percent of the total population. By 2020, the prediction goes, there will be more than forty million elderly.

This present graying of America is due primarily to factors which began to have their effect at the beginning of this century — a dramatic reduction in infant mortality, better nutrition, and more readily available health care facilities. These factors combined to enable those babies born during a birth boom after the turn of the century to survive in unprecedented numbers. For the future, the present declining birthrate, which is the consequence of the increase in women choosing careers rather than child bearing, of legalized abortion and the accessibility of contraception, means that the percentage of older persons in the total population will

Introducing a Brighter Shade of Gray

increase as the children of the post World War II baby boom become old. Given the powerful thrust of the present trends, it doesn't seem likely that there will be another rise in the birthrate within the next fifty years. America is definitely getting older.

People are also living longer. At the turn of the century the average age expectancy was fifty. Today it is seventy-one. Now a person reaching the age of sixty-five can expect to live for an additional fifteen years, and the percentage of people living past eighty is steadily rising. Moreover, many researchers believe that if sufficient funds were devoted to the task, they could probably learn enough about the aging process to extend life expectancy almost ten more years by the end of the century.

If America seems increasingly to be a country of old people, it is not yet a country *for* them. False myths and negative stereotypes about aging prevail among most Americans and have an impact on the well-being of the elderly. The stereotypes become a lumping process that denies older people their individuality. It considers them all alike, rather than as individuals with different levels of physical and mental functioning. A reading of the Harris Poll of 1975* suggests that most younger Americans believe that older Americans are friendly at their best, but basically are poor, sexless, physically impaired, intellectually failed and incompetent. In short, a group of twenty-three million people who properly belong in nursing homes.

Let's look at some facts. A harsh one is that approximately twenty-three percent of the elderly live in households that are near or at the poverty level. Yet many of them receive food stamps, Medicaid, can have a free meal at a nutrition site and do get some financial assistance from their children. While poverty is certainly painful and a serious problem for several million people, the majority of the elderly are not destitute and do get along financially. An interesting statistic is that seventy-nine percent of elderly couples and fifty percent of the men and women living alone own the homes they live in, which implies better than terrible poverty.

One fact that invariably evokes surprise — a response that illustrates how little we know about aging in America — is that less than five percent of the elderly are in nursing homes. There are serious health problems. Eighteen percent of the elderly living in households have chronic ailments that limit their mobility and functioning. The majority of them are over seventy-five. However, an accurate picture of America's elderly population would show that most of them are in good enough shape to jog, swim, ride bikes, dance, play doubles, work, garden and do whatever they like. Furthermore, they're better off being active in these ways. Those elderly who don't exercise should. They can do so without fear of collapsing, and as a matter of fact, a planned, reasonable program of exercise would improve their physical well-being astonishingly and impede decline.

What should be welcome and reassuring information, since Amer-

---

*"The Myth and Reality of Aging in America"—A Study for The National Council on the Aging Inc. by Louis Harris & Associates Inc. 1976.

icans of all ages share some worries about sex, is that the capacity for sexual gratification does not end with the initial Social Security check. It's lifelong.

As for the idea that an older person's mind vanishes with time, it's time that notion vanished. There is no shrinking or destruction of brain cells in normal aging until at least ninety years old, and not necessarily then. Nor is there any loss of intelligence or learning ability. Some tests indicate that it takes older persons a longer time than it does younger people to solve arithmetic problems. This is most likely due to the stress of the unusual testing situation (it's been many years since the average sixty-five-year-old took a final exam), as well as the fact that they don't practice the necessary skills very often.

As we well know from the experiences of minority groups — and the elderly are no exception — negative stereotypes cause considerable human misery. And when the victims accept society's distorted images as accurate representations of who they are, then the trouble is compounded. As long as they are not exposed, the stereotypes will continue and subsequent generations of elderly will regard themselves with disfavor, believing what they learned when they were younger. That's what's going on now.

Understandably, this situation frequently has a bad effect among the elderly on their self-esteem, confidence and the will to explore new possibilities. For example, an older person who had tuned into the popular myth that the elderly deteriorate intellectually and can't learn would probably not make use of the chance to go to college for fear of being unable to do the work and be thought of as a stupid old person.

Gerontologists have coined the term "Ageism" to indicate prejudice against the old simply for being old. In our society, which overvalues youth, the forms this prejudice has taken are obvious — as in compulsory retirement for workers — and latent, as in our neglect and ignorance of matters concerning older Americans. A term such as Ageism is a useful tool, the resourceful women's movement having taught us the technique of consciousness-raising. It compels us to examine our attitudes and to reflect on how to change what needs changing.

While Ageism is still the bee in the lives of older Americans, its sting is easing somewhat. The times are definitely changing — maybe not fast enough — but definitely changing. Literally millions of older persons, refusing to lead lives of extreme quietism, have formed and shaped powerful organizations that work effectively for them. The leadership is sophisticated and experienced in the do's and don't's of power, wise in the chess moves of political action, and has the know-how to make friends with unfriendly Congressmen. Another good thing has been the emergence within the last twenty-five years of approximately three hundred national organizations that deal with programs relating to the elderly. Through research, scholarship, networks of communication and the very weight of

Introducing a Brighter Shade of Gray

their prestige they have exerted an enormous influence on the study of gerontology, which hardly anyone even knew how to spell before World War II. Result — a body of valuable and available knowledge about a previously uninvestigated subject. One could say that the spread of this new understanding of the elderly among private institutions, professionals working in the field, organizations of the elderly and congressional committees convinced the federal government that it should intervene.

This year the bottom line of that intervention is at least several billion dollars (the exact figure is difficult to determine because much revenue is available that is not specifically earmarked for the elderly) and provides money for a variety of services and programs: housing, meals, research, training, home care, recreation, senior centers, jobs, transportation and volunteers — just to name a few. While not exactly the millennium, since many needs of the most needy elderly people will still not be met, progress has been spectacular. In 1965, when Congress passed the Older American Act, the initial funding was $7.5 million. Quite a difference between then and now!

That initial funding seems to have been an expression of both indifference and contempt on the part of our nation's lawmakers. Yet, it is not difficult to understand when one recalls that in 1965 America was in the midst of a greening process and youth was truth. Ironically, many of the young themselves, those who were part of the counterculture, viewed the elderly sympathetically. They saw them as indifferent to values of productivity and economic status, which they too rejected. But their parents, the middle generation that shared society's values, were the ones who reacted to the heightened emphasis on youth and became more anxious about becoming old.

However, the tremendous leap in government spending since 1965 reflects a changing societal attitude despite the prevalence of Ageism. The efforts of the elderly themselves, gerontologists and other workers in the field of aging are key factors in this change. Another is the growing awareness among the middle-aged that there is less and less traditional work to do in America as technology's wheels keep turning. Many of them are victims of this development — unneeded workers — while others see it as their potential fate. This has made them less prone to deny aging as a reality and more able to identify with the elderly as individual human beings with whom they may already have a great deal in common.

While the transitional attitude is confused and uncertain, it nonetheless acknowledges that the elderly have a place in American life. Exactly what and where that place is remains to be discovered — by young and old alike. At any rate, if the questions are here, can the answers be far behind?

One crucial problem facing the elderly is what they are to do with their new leisure. Some received it though not wanting it, while others wanted it at first, but then found it wanting. For both groups, the time on their hands may make them restless, troubled and dissatisfied, the golden years of retirement bringing more problems than pleasures. Of course there are many older persons who knew the answer without even asking the question, and we can learn a great deal about successful aging from them.

As human beings, we seek to do what is both meaningful and worthwhile to us in order to feel good about ourselves. This presents a problem for the elderly, who it seems are not expected by the rest of society to do anything and, as a result, frequently don't know what to do. Being useful is one of the basics for a life of felt meaning, but again that is very difficult for the elderly to accomplish in our society, which has always defined *useful* as *working* for men and *raising a family* for women.

The elderly themselves can generate much of the thrust that will open the bright doors to life's satisfactions. To gain the respected place in society to which they are entitled, they must employ the lively arts of example, persuasion and demand. They must resist the pressures of Ageism from the outside and from their own nagging inner voices, which will sometimes echo the worst messages society is sending out. Not easy, but not impossible, the kind of endeavor that gives one the juice to wake up each morning, knowing who's up and deserves a smile in the mirror.

This book contains examples of older persons who refuse to accept the non-roles society has thus far assigned them and who are enjoying their old age. In some cases, they are finding it the best time of their lives.

Some who reject the notion that retirement is appropriate for everyone at age sixty-five or seventy continue to do the work that has brought them status, stimulation and an income for many years. They are fortunate in knowing what they want and need and in being able to hold on to it. But not all work is necessarily worth doing. Actually, the evidence indicates that a good job nowadays is hard to find. If work is dull, tedious, boring, repetitive, oppressive, senseless and merely endured, then one is wise to welcome retirement. And that's when the effort to find something better than the dreary past one has left behind should begin. Otherwise there will be fresh data for an old age stereotype. Retiring does not merely mean going to sleep.

Another meaning of retiring is "changing position," a sensible way for older persons to define the end of those habits and rituals fashioned by many years of 9:00 to 5:00 living. The definition indicates that there is a view of life available other than the accustomed one, a view which could offer a landscape of greener grass. Retired and without the pressures of competition, achievement and limited time that the world of work imposes, older people have an opportunity to explore interests and involve themselves in new activities, both for their intrinsic worth and for the sake of their own personal growth.

The idea of personal growth as a possibility for older people has gained credibility only within the past few years, despite the fact that the idea has been considered relevant for other Americans for about twenty-five years. The delay, another example of Ageism, was rationalized by the refrain, "They're too old to change. It's a waste of time and effort."

It's cruel and rather absurd to claim that older persons are not capable of changing, of gaining a better understanding of themselves, others and the world around them. That's growth, and it results in people behaving and doing things that will bring them more satisfaction. For the elderly there are many roads to choose from on this journey.

There are discussion groups at senior centers, colleges, churches and social agencies, where older people can express their feelings and attitudes about everything from gray hair to grandchildren and discover better ways of relating to others. For those who feel very depressed or overwhelmed, individual and group psychotherapy are obtainable and have proven successful. The arts are still a perennial source of enrichment and are available to the elderly. New programs designed for them, as well as performances at reduced rates, make it possible for the elderly to be extensively involved as either audience or art makers. Through the arts, older persons can gain a deepened sense of life and meaning and a fresh pleasure in the sounds, colors and shapes of the breathing world. If practicing artists, they can experience the timeless satisfactions of creating and recreating themselves in their work.

Learning is growth. In recent years the educational establishment, responding to the demographic facts of life, the declining numbers of college-aged youth and the rising numbers of elderly, has shifted gears. Today universities and colleges all over the country have established a cornucopia of programs to meet the educational needs of the elderly. They can return to campus and complete the unfinished business of getting the degree they had put aside for whatever reasons, or start working toward a first, second or third degree. They can prepare for a new career or enjoy the rare luxury of learning for learning's sake. Besides the fortresses of higher education, there are community centers, Y's, and adult education centers that offer older people the chance to try their hands at a variety of do-it-yourself courses. Whether learning how to repair the kitchen sink or getting the piano back in tune, the feelings of accomplishment and increased self-sufficiency are worth the low cost of admission.

Helping others, giving of oneself to those who need it, is a basic human impulse that older persons can fulfill. Private organizations, as well as churches, hospitals and schools, actively seek the volunteer services of the elderly to assist people of all ages. There are also several government-funded programs that hire older persons as helpers for the frail elderly. Whatever the assistance — as expert advisor, teacher, chore aid or friendly companion — the elderly who involve themselves derive rich feelings of connection and intimacy. They gain a precious sense of usefulness that vitalizes living and provides an unquestioned purpose for it.

Introducing a Brighter Shade of Gray

Another good way to spark the spirit is to raise the human voice in protest and assertion. Several million of the elderly, aware that debate and decision-making are not esoteric arts, have joined political organizations comprised of older persons. Exclaiming their outrage at being ignored and unjustly treated by the government, joining together for their common good, older activists have either regained or acquired an exhilarating strength. They have observed that strength in action on many occasions, having moved lawmakers to pass the legislation they wanted. Gray power is more fact than slogan, and those elderly who participate, create it, share it and do not feel themselves powerless victims of society.

The company of one's peers and the opportunity to communicate the small details and significant events of daily living with those whose situation is like one's own — these sweets of socializing — are the good reasons why millions of elderly all over the country attend senior centers. For both those living alone and those who live with spouses, the center is a hummingly alive place where they can find companionship, good food and a smorgasboard of cultural, recreational and educational activities. Many elderly persons, previously lonely, depressed and without any stimulation in their lives, joined centers and were recharged. They found new interests, discovered aptitudes and developed skills in an environment where they are the most important persons, rather than the least. At the senior center, the elderly are truly at the center.

While senior centers restore precious feelings of community, one strong private need which many elderly people want to satisfy remains. It is the need to share life intimately with just one other person, as in marriage. There are over six million elderly who in their later years have lost spouses through death or divorce, but there are pressures and problems, expecially for women, that do not lead to high numbers of remarriages. Nevertheless, there were at least thirty-three thousand marriages of older people in 1976. Though society may be critical of their decisions, the elderly who remarry love one another, enjoy sex and frequently find more happiness than in previous marriages. A loving marriage offers older people the same thing it does for the young, a shared future shaped in the yeast of caring and belonging. However, marriage has a special quality for the elderly. Their abundant leisure time enables them to wake up to slow, delicate mornings and the promise of long days together.

Continuing to work, finding new careers, going back to school, volunteering, becoming politically active, attending senior centers, remarrying — these are the significant ways that many of the elderly have chosen to continue their lives as self-esteeming human beings. Hopefully, these chosen ways are stepping-stones that other older persons can also follow to a more desirable place and time than here and now. Nor does it seem unreasonable to anticipate a future when society will readily grant its longest-lived members a large degree of status and even honor.

Introducing a Brighter Shade of Gray

Appropriately, it is older people who are supplying much of the dynamic leadership that is necessary to effect a change from the invidious present. Like superstars anywhere, the most prominent leaders among the elderly exude a charismatic brilliance. They highlight a vision of the better future while helping to achieve it.

Three of them, Ollie Randall, Nelson Cruikshank and Maggie Kuhn, each differing in personality and action style, are renowned in the field of aging and admired by literally millions of elderly people. Nevertheless, most Americans would probably fail to identify them on a "Who's Who" quiz. This curious invisibility, which could be termed sociological magic, is actually not a mystery. It is but another example of how Ageism determines what we see and fail to see.

Yet it is difficult to accept the fact that someone as durable and successful as Ollie Randall, who has been dealing with issues concerning the elderly for more than fifty years, could remain so unrecognized by the vast majority of her fellow citizens. Many in the field refer to her as a living legend, and one is even tempted to call her the Grandmother of Aging. Giant spirit in an elfin body, Ollie started in the 1920s to initiate programs that are now institutions, such as vacations for the poor elderly, housing for healthy, functioning older people and the senior center. She also helped formulate Social Security legislation. Modest about her achievements, Ollie seems unaware of her own gifts. While ordinary taxpayers see the world about them as inevitable and permanent, she has a different view. Ollie has one of those unusual sensibilities which, looking at present circumstances, perceives the necessity for change, imagines the forms that change should take and then tries to bring them about. History illustrates that such daring often leads to a sad ending, but Ollie continued to lecture, write, advise and travel everywhere well into her eighth decade.

Nelson Cruikshank, recently appointed by President Carter as the first Counsellor on Aging in the nation's history, is impressive as both symbol and man. The President's action of adding an advisor on aging to his White House circle symbolized a commitment to new priorities. Matters relating to aging would no longer be shunted to the rear of the national bus. Raised in rural Ohio, Mr. Cruikshank worked as a youth on ore ships that traveled the Great Lakes, and he was later educated for the ministry; his roots are nineteenth-century traditional American, nurtured in the soil of values that stressed hard work and service to others. His life story recalls a time of moral certainty in the country, which exists now only as nostalgia.

During his career, Mr. Cruikshank directed programs for the poor, for the government and for the AFL-CIO. He was elected to the presidency of the National Council of Senior Citizens' 3,500,000-member organization in 1969. From then until his recent appointment, Nelson Cruikshank was an articulate, tireless spokesman. Frequently consulted by members of Congress, he was perhaps the most conspicuous advocate for older persons in the nation. On several levels then, his move from NCSC headquarters in downtown Washington to the Executive Office Building near the White House was not a difficult journey.

Maggie Kuhn refers to herself as a "wrinkled radical," a name which has charmed the media and was probably calculated to do just that, for Maggie, who initiated the Gray Panther organization, has a shrewd understanding of winning tactics. She knows how to dramatize an issue, utilizing techniques that are in part derived from the political street theater of the 1960s and part the expression of her ebullient, feisty spirit — while all parts attract attention to her cause.

Maggie is a fiery speaker whose ample indignation fuels her rhetoric of denunciation and demand. She wants nothing less than a total transformation of society's treatment of older people, and she urges all the elderly to insist on that transformation as vigorously as she does.

An avowed activist, Maggie recognizes that society will not alter its ways without considerable pressure, which she's ready to exert with the help of friends, both young and old. The determined spirit of this woman as it flashes in speech or interview often elicits startled admiration. The expectation is that an old woman with a passionate cause should be running around in sneakers and be somewhat eccentric. But Maggie Kuhn is undeniably cogent and as relevant as the issues she argues.

Ollie Randall, who represents the pioneer achievements, the vital tradition in the field of aging, Nelson Cruikshank, who symbolizes the new dignity and status that the movement has attained, and Maggie Kuhn, prophet of its future direction — these are truly a "big three."

New York, New York

Ollie Randall—Age 86

Life was better for old people in America at the turn of the century. At least that's what I remember. I was brought up in a family with a great many older people. My great-grandmother, my two great-aunts and my grandparents. We all lived in a kind of compound: my family in a small house, my grandparents in a larger house, and these were all on the same grounds. There wasn't any antagonism because they were old. My grandfather worked until he was seventy-five with no problems at a very important job in Providence. My great-aunts weren't as active, but if one of them ever needed anything, she came to our house. It was just part of the practice of our family to help each other out and keep together. When my Aunt Sara needed a cataract operation and had to convalesce, there was no question but that we children would move out of our bedroom so she could use it. One of my chores as a child was to take daily coffee to my great-grandmother, and I loved it and I loved her. I always got along with them and liked them. So I grew up in this milieu in which the older people were respected or cared for and consulted about things that ought to be done or not be done.

I actually saw that change. When I first started working after college, I sensed the shifting of the mores, or at least the family mores. When I went into public welfare work, I found that one of the things that the welfare system had done was to destroy the family, the possibility of several generations living together. These rulings, that if older people lived with their adult children they couldn't have any public assistance even though they needed it, did more to cause the disintegration of the family than anything else. I worked hard trying to have those rules and regulations changed, but without success. I tried to tell the federal agency I was working with at the time they did that cruel thing, that it was socially wrong; economically, you would have to figure it out, but socially it was wrong. I still believe it.

I was out in St. Louis recently at a rally of about three hundred older people. We were having a discussion about housing. A Baptist minister came in to listen and made the comment that most people today are breaking the commandment of honoring your mother and father by not keeping them in their homes. I said, "You may be right, but I wonder if you have stopped to think that the ways you honored your mother and father haven't changed radically during the centuries, while the conditions of the family have changed." I asked how many of the people in the room had adult children in their families. Practically everybody in the audience raised their hands. Then I asked how many lived with their children. Three people raised their hands. Then I asked how many of them would prefer to live with their children if they could. Not a hand went up. The three people who had raised their hands probably would have been a lot happier if they hadn't been living with their children. We have to start working much more strongly on the integration of generations now; this emphasis on disintegration is all wrong. I happen to believe rather firmly that there can be family ties, but you don't have to be in the same house if your relationships are sound and friendly and the people care about each other. This is so vital, not only for the older person, but for the younger person as well. And this whole thing was brought about by economic concerns entirely. First the public welfare system set up that terrible ruling. And the first thing you knew, you had older people living alone and other people living on their own.

When I was down in Washington in the thirties with Harry Hopkins, Frances Perkins and the rest, what we were trying primarily to do was establish a financial underpinning for older people in their retirement years. We weren't trying to do a social service job; we weren't trying to do anything but an economic one. That was the original aim of the whole Social Security Act — to see that people had a basic amount of money that they could count on, much of which would come because it was put in while they were working. We tried to build into the whole system of payment and retirement planning. At first they said the age of retirement would be seventy. This was in the Depression, and when the staff looked at the statistics, they saw that the seventy-year-old cutoff wouldn't take enough people out of the market to give jobs to younger people. It was reduced to sixty-five because Bismarck did it in Germany. I said the only reason he did it over there was that nobody was going to live to be more than sixty-five, so he didn't have any trouble. Sixty-five was just an arbitrary decision based on the economics of the Depression. Before this whole darn business of Social Security started, people just tended to keep on working. At that time there weren't the same attitudes we have today about old people working. They may have been thought of as negligible and not amounting to much, but they weren't thought of as people who couldn't be in the labor market. There was no antagonism about years at the time. That has of course changed. And I think we're responsible for that because of the way we handled the economics of the Depression, just using a statistical guess to get older people out of the work force.

I was always concerned about support for the elderly, though. I was in there from the beginning, from 1916 on. I was interested in getting them enough money to live in their own homes. When we had a chance to have a home for the aged, of course we used it. But the thing that I found most fascinating was that there was such a demand for a decent place to live. We had a waiting list from here to Christmas. I managed to get some money from several foundations to help me support these people while they were waiting. This taught me a great deal in the course of working with the waiting list. It was home care we needed, not institutional care. Home care is the alternative to institutions. When I first started working with the elderly, I was in personnel. I worked with the elderly just because I liked it, for example, not by planning for it. I found that none of the social workers could get along with old people and had a very difficult time interviewing them. I was just friendly. In fact, I wrote an article, "Dare to be Friendly." But I've always worked with extraordinary people, from those I met in my first job in educational research in Boston as well as the president of the agency where I worked for for such a long time. Our agency ran a workshop for older people; we put them to work five days a week and we found jobs wherever we could fit them in. Hopefully, we would be able to keep people in their own homes, from the money that they earned themselves.

Institutional care had always been the alternative to home care before I got into the field. Now today we're beginning to recognize that people want to stay in their own homes. There's been a shift. And you know who's responsible for this shift? The older people. The older people aren't begging for these institutional favors. They're asking for something that will help them go on living in their own homes.

My first job full time with the elderly was in running a home in upstate New York. There was a wealthy man who had heard about the work my agency was doing with older people. He had an estate up on the Hudson that he wanted to turn into a home for older people, and he felt that our agency was the organization to do it. I had been the assistant to the administrator and was very nervous about running this whole thing by myself. But in any case, the agency was given a thousand acres of land with a big house, and we started a home for the aged up there in Dutchess County. We had the summer vacation place for old people, cottages, camps for young people, nursing home patients and so forth. After a lot of reorganization at the agency, I was asked by the director of the agency to ·be his own assistant on programs on aging. Not just in our agency but in voluntary agencies across the country. The next thing I knew, I was traveling all over the place. So I started out doing some fieldwork on aging in voluntary agencies throughout the country. This gave me a lot of good experience. All these social service agencies were very eager to start programs for the elderly. After the Social Security legislation was passed, people in social service realized that it was not enough just to support people economically. Money just wasn't enough. That's why I regret the whole Social Security thing, tying it up with social services. I happen to believe it would have been better to have left it plain economics.

But today I have no problems getting people to listen to me, and I've had extraordinarily good experiences lately. I've been talking to people all over the country and abroad about the fact that older people are increasing in numbers, increasing in awareness and increasing in their understanding about what they can do for themselves. They understand that working together towards the ends will be most meaningful for them as well as to others. They're not entirely selfish in this. What benefits old people will in the long run benefit everybody. Whether or not they believe it, young people are going to be old someday, too.

I've found this new awareness in various countries, like Nigeria, France and Greece. I've just been to Greece, in fact. Even in the developing countries, they're recognizing that with the increasing numbers of older people the gap between the old and young is a social and political situation that they have to deal with. People are getting old all over the world, not just in the United States and Canada. It's happening more and more. The life expectancy has so increased for so many people in so many countries that their governments are realizing that they have to come to grips with the problems of the elderly. We're just not dying off the way we used to. Just look at me.

At Vichy, I gave the summarization speech at a meeting with representatives from twenty countries. It was an amazing opportunity to be there with all these people from all these different countries and find them all facing this problem of numbers and lack of social and political means to take care of them. I told them they were one of the few outfits I had ever heard of that let a woman have the last word. The field has grown and I was there early.

People still listen to me when they have to. I've always been able to communicate with large groups, expecially groups of elderly people. That's probably because I'm one of them. It's not like I'm some youngster telling them how to do something. They know I'm in the same boat as they are and we all have the same situation to face. But that's how it always was for me. I always felt very close to the people I was working with. It's a little different now because I'm not officially employed anywhere. Whatever I do, I do on my own or at the request of some agency. I don't have any professional concerns, worrying about offending so-and-so at some agency, anymore. I haven't had a paying job since 1965, and so you can see I'm getting along quite nicely without official employment.

I was forced to retire. My agency had compulsory retirement at sixty-five, but they kept me on for three years as a consultant. Now and then I still consult with them on this, that or the other thing. But I'm glad not to be in an agency; you're so much freer. I went to work with them in 1916, and so I think I've had enough. I've never had the feeling of being irrelevant or too old to be consulted on things. I speak in lots of different places, as long as they pay my expenses, of course. But I guess I've been in the field so long that I'm a habit. At this point, this field is my life, and if I can be useful to others and get other older people to get concerned enough about themselves to do something about it, I'm satisfied.

The major things that I want to see changed now are matters of attitude. I think we're getting to the point where we're able to persuade the public that getting old doesn't mean you're going to be witless or helpless or anything else. I think older people are beginning to demonstrate that there is validity in the fact that you can be a person as long as you live. All you have to do is keep yourself healthy, both physically and mentally. Old people themselves are going to be the ones who prove this.

But I have never had plans, except to take a secretarial course when I got out of college. The things that have happened have happened. I just live day to day.

Washington, D.C.

Nelson Cruikshank—Age 75

When I was young, I was very fortunate to be part of an extended family. My grandmother and grandfather lived on a farm in Ohio that my uncle ran. I spent most of my summers on this Ohio farm. When I was a kid eight or ten years old, my grandparents were already in their early seventies, but they were still very lively. I also knew my grandparents on my mother's side well. We spent Christmas and Thanksgiving on each of the old family homesteads. It was a very traditional family situation, like the kind you see on picture postcards. I lived in a kind of protected, wonderful atmosphere, where my grandfather was regarded as an austere man. He didn't have the flowing white whiskers, but he was very vigorous. In his eighties he was still chopping wood, doing a full day's work. We all loved, revered and respected him. My grandfather was ninety-six when I was a young man with a child; he and my grandmother knew their grandchildren.

So you see, I know how it ought to be, even though I realize that social conditions are different, and there aren't many Ohio farms left in which the son can take over and the old man be around to counsel and give advice. This picture gives perhaps the best recollection of old age. I think one facet of the breakdown of the family is that respect for old people has eroded. I don't think the family has completely broken down, but the sense of the three-generation family isn't with us nearly as much as it was. I think part of this is due to our highly industrialized and highly mobile society. The children and the grandchildren just don't live around the nuclear family like they did. They've moved to the West Coast, the East Coast and the Midwest. When the automobile industry exploded, the children moved away to the North.

In a young and expanding nation, there is inevitably a certain premium on youth. During all the expansion years, especially the first two decades of this century, business was expanding, opportunities were expanding, and the world belonged to the young, the vigorous, the inventive. In that kind of society, the old were thought to be in the way. Here was a horse-and-buggy age rapidly turning into an automobile age. What could the old folks do? The generation born during the later span of my life has seen more change than any other generation in a thousand years. If you look back from the beginning of the Christian era to the beginning of the

Nelson Cruikshank

Renaissance period, you will find fewer changes in these fourteen hundred years than in the last seventy. The Wright Brothers flew about half the length of a 747 six months after I was born. That was the first heavier-than-air machine that had ever taken off the ground, and that was in my lifetime. Now if you have the money you can be in London in three hours. In the midst of all this rapid change, it's the young people who can quickly adapt to new ideas. I think it's the rapidly changing times and the sophisticated modes of transportation which make it easier for people to move that account for the nuclear family breaking up.

I don't think I attribute it to any unique hardheartedness on the part of the American people. We can all contrast our civilization and attitudes to the older Orientals. Well, they haven't changed their lives the way we have. Take China. Sure, there's been a revolution, but not the kind of revolution that we've had. How many automobiles are there in China? How many sons and daughters move and set up a family 3,000 miles away? Sure there are big industrial centers, but it's still largely an agrarian, family unit kind of situation. The older people there occupy a place similar to the one my grandfather did. If China becomes highly industrialized, they may lose that kind of veneration for their older people the way we lost it. I don't know; it's *the* part of their culture. Perhaps we can hope for the Chinese that if they do change, they won't change as rapidly as we did. We did it awfully fast.

Again, as far as my own family goes I was very fortunate. I had only one child, but she had six children. So she made up for the rest of us. They don't live too far away, in Philadelphia, so we are together very often. In fact we spend our vacations together. We've taken a cruise boat, the whole bunch of us, and cruised for ten days. We have wonderful times together. My grandchildren come down and stay with me for a week at a time. There is a continuing sense of family. This is also true with my two sisters. One passed away, but before that we were always getting together back at the old homestead in Ohio where our cousins are still living. It's a big mob when we all get together. I consider myself very lucky. Nothing pleases me more than the fact that my twenty-two-year-old granddaughter will come down here and stay with me for a couple of weeks. She's now at Yellowstone Park with a job, and as soon as she lands there, she writes me a letter. Everyone uses the telephone, but it's not the same.

I wish that unity could be for everybody. Some people associate old age only with lingering illness and senility and so forth; this is a very different picture from mine. My picture of old age was perhaps not typical, but it was a very positive one. I carried a kind of respect for old age from my childhood into my adulthood. This experience might have influenced my going into the field of aging.

I think there are two significant things about my appointment as Counsellor on Aging. First, there has never been anything like that before. There has never been someone to advise the President on matters relating to older people right on the White House staff. But there's a second significance. Before the President appointed me Counsellor on Aging, he appointed me as chairman of the fifteen-member federal council set up to make recommendations to the President on all matters affecting the aging and to oversee the government agencies with jurisdiction in that area. This means that the job as Counsellor can be more than the job of personal advisor. The significance of the two jobs being combined is that I bring to the President more than just my own views and recommendations. For instance, I can say to him, "Mr. President, this is the consensus of fifteen broadly representative people coming from a number of organizations and backgrounds, including different academic backgrounds and disciplines." I think that that statement will have a lot more force than one coming from one advisor. So to my mind there's a kind of double-edged significance there.

It's a little early to tell how this job compares to my other jobs. The scope is broader, and maybe the impact is a little more blunt. Now what this job entails is seeing that when a policy is up for consideration at the highest level of the government, the impact of that policy on people will be known to the President. It doesn't mean, and it can't possibly mean, that that will then be the only consideration. Suppose he has a tax proposal before him. Maybe somebody in Congress has a proposal to change the age of the double exemption. I'll see that there is before him a study of the impact of that on older people, particularly retired people. Since that example is a little remote, take one like Social Security. There the impact is very direct. I'll tell him that if this policy is adopted it will have this effect on older people. It may be a good effect, it may be a bad effect, it may be a mixed effect. I'll say to him, "Mr. President, this is what it will do to older people. Just be sure that in your computer this is part of your input." Of course I will make that as forceful as I can, recognizing that it can't be the only determining factor. There are many factors that the President will have to take into account.

Let's say there was a Presidential policy I didn't agree with. I would play a different role from when I was heading a private organization. There you could blast away and say whatever you felt. But as long as you're part of a team, you let your position be known and go along with the top decision, recognizing there are other factors in the decision. Once in a rare while, a thing becomes a matter of very basic principles.

If you're asked to support something in which you really don't believe, then you ask yourself, "How significant is this? Does it really compromise my principles?" If it does, then you get off the team. You don't go around with a chip on your shoulder and keep saying, "Well you don't play my way so I'll pick up my dollies and go home." Whenever you're part of any basic institution, it has to be a critical issue in which you feel a basic principle is involved which compromises you. I don't expect anything like this to happen. But you always have in mind that there's always that possibility. You reserve the right to maintain your own integrity.

The unique part about this appointment is that it's never before been one person's primary responsibility. Other people have sometimes done it but always as a sort of side issue to their other jobs. The job's a two-way street in that it will be one of my responsibilities to present and explain to both government people and people in the private sector what the presidential program is. Right now he has a very forward-looking program financing the Social Security system. He's strengthening that system. It's a good program, but a lot of people don't understand it. I'll be making speeches about it, explaining it and trying to whip up support for it.

There are many problems of old age that need to be confronted. Certainly one of the most serious belongs to the group we call the frail elderly. As fortunate as you may be to be healthy at the age of seventy-five, you know there is going to be a time of declining health and declining activity even before you get to the point where you need institutional or other support. You know there is going to be a time when gradually you can't do the things that you did. I look forward with dread, for example, to the time when I can't drive. Things that I like to do depend upon that freedom of motion. Yet I know it will come one of these days, and then what will I do?

What do you do, when you're no longer independent but need continuing supportive care? This is a problem we haven't solved individually or familywise. What happens when a couple can't support each other or if one of the partners is gone and the other doesn't want to go back and be a burden on the children? That does something to a family relationship, no matter how wholesome it is. That is one of the things that is very, very serious. We haven't got a policy for that in this country yet. We're working on it, trying to get one developed.

Then of course there's the immense fear of being put in a nursing home that hangs over every older person's head like the sword of Damocles. Not to mention the whole matter of financing this care. It has to be determined what is properly public responsibility and what part is individual or family responsibility. We don't have these answers yet because these are very baffling problems.

Of course the problems vary for different people. You look at the figures and see that the problems of widowhood are very different from the problems of men who lose their wives. Actually in many ways older men get along even better than older women. Somehow or other it's assumed by the sons and daughters that the man is more helpless than the woman, and they often take him in more readily than they take in Mother. That seems an anomaly, but it's often the case. Men are sometimes more gregarious than women. That is, during their earlier lifetime they often had more contact out among workers, companions, etc., than women did. Women in the past tended to rely on smaller social circles confined to family and friends. Add to this the fact that women tend to live so much longer, and by the time you get up into the eighties, you'll find there are three women to every two men. So I think there are more lonely old women than there are lonely old men, although there are many of both. Then our income-maintenance programs are not so well designed for women as they are for men. Pension plans often have a survivor benefit plan. But despite odds that the wife will outlive the husband, our pension plans are designed as if the man will outlive the woman. Because he's been on the payroll, the plan's attached to his work record. So the level of income of older widows is another very serious problem. But it is something that we can do something about.

Now on the other hand, there is a kind of general cultural attitude in this country that when a person reaches age sixty or sixty-five he's over the hill; he's had it. I haven't personally experienced any prejudice from younger people in my day to day working and social life. But maybe I'm oblivious to it. I'm a pretty brash guy. I've never been bashful, and in fact I laugh it off in advance if I come into a room where there are a lot of younger guys. I say, "Well, here I am, the oldest guy in the room, and that means I get the most comfortable chair in the room whether there are any women around or not." And I take it.

Yet I must say there's a slight attitude around this young administration. Occasionally I observe it when we begin to talk about our experience in government. You see, I had experience in government before I went to the AFL-CIO, in some of the New Deal agencies. I notice that once in a while when I start to say, "This is the way we did it back in the thirties," there's kind of a benevolent smile, as if to say, "Well, that's okay, pop, but what does that have to do with our problems?" Well, I think one does have something to do with the other. And maybe there's something to be learned. It's true that when people get up against really sticky problems, they are more inclined to listen. Anyway, my feeling is that if an idea or an angle has merit, its turn will come, and if it doesn't, then it should be discarded.

In regard to the scope of some of the difficulties of government, there are times when I'm discouraged, of course. But oddly enough it's often young people I see getting more discouraged than we older people do. It dawned on me one time why it was. I had a brilliant young staff at the AFL-CIO when I was over there during one of our big drives. At the time I was about sixty-two. We came within two votes of getting Medicare passed in the Senate. We were pretty sure that if we got it passed in the Senate we'd get it passed in the House, and then we lost by two votes after months of intensive work. I came back from the Hill where I watched the voting in the gallery of the Senate, and found one of my brilliant young Phi Beta Kappa economists in tears. I said to her, "You can't win 'em all," and she said to me, "All this work gone for nothing." All of a sudden, it dawned on me. There she is, probably twenty-eight or twenty-nine years old, and she's never had a victory. I can always look back to those glorious days of the New Deal when bang! bang! bang! we were getting one thing after another. So a blow like that I could see as a kind of temporary setback. And I've seen it happen since then. My twenty-two-year-old granddaughter is more apt to become gloomy than I am. I see this, then I think. She was in her teens at the time of the Vietnam War, and she has never been old enough to be politically conscious at a time when the liberal forces won a national election. Every one that she had seen has been lost. Like the kids on my staff, she's never seen a victory. I hope she does before too long. So I do see some of the younger people as more despairing sometimes than my peers. You should see *us* when we get together in a convention or something. We really shake the rafters.

The issues are very complex now. These victories I referred to were forward movements. We didn't have the problem of running out of energy. There was no scarcity of things even in the Depression. It was just that things were not distributed properly. Now we're running up against problems like overpopulation and genuine scarcity. What is the answer? I think part of the present malaise is due to the fact that problems are tremendously more complex and answers are not readily at hand, even though the young know much more about the world in their teens and twenties than I did at that age. Still it's the unanswerables that really weigh down on people of all ages right now. Life is demanding.

Somehow I always seem to have the energy to keep up with my very busy schedule. I am a little more tired and sleepy than I used to be. I used to do a full day's work and then sit up and read half the night. I don't do that anymore. I find that I take a good book, decide that I'm going to read, and the first thing I know, I'm asleep. I don't run out of energy during the day. In day-to-day work, I have no problems. But who could expect to have at seventy-five what they had at forty? I miss those long evenings of reading, but I adjust to it. Lots of times I work at the office from 6:00 to 10:00 at night. Sure, I get home tired, sort of run out of gas. But if I get a good night's sleep, I'm all right the next day. I guess I attribute my good health, my physical stamina and energy to two things. First, good inheritance and second, the fact that my mother and father were always very conscious of our health and well-being when we were growing up. They provided us with a good environment and a protected childhood, although I don't think that always assures longevity or stamina.

The doctors told me it's inheritance as much as anything. You either have the good genes or you don't. I think I inherit most of my genes from my grandfather on my mother's side, the old man I was telling you about. I didn't get them all from him, but I got enough that I consider myself lucky.

For nine years preceding my appointment as Counsellor on Aging I was president of the National Council of Senior Citizens. That's a federation of some thirty-eight hundred clubs and centers in every state in the Union. But that was a volunteer job. Going back just before that, I was a visiting professor at three universities: Michigan State, Penn State, and University of Michigan. Those were one-term appointments, because I was supposedly retired. For twenty-two years, with a break of one year, I was director of the Social Security Department of the AFL-CIO. Of course that got me into the problems of older people because I dealt with the legislative field. You could say that I was a lobbyist. I worked in the field of social security and health security. I also dealt with pension plans and negotiated health plans with the unions affiliated with the AFL-CIO. So for some twenty-two years I have been dealing with the problems of older workers and retired persons. It was a kind of natural lead-in to this appointment.

I would like to finish up with this job. I thought I was through with active life before it came along. I was active in the campaign, and I told my friends that after that I was going to resign from the National Council and catch up with my reading and a few other things that I wanted to do. But then this came along, and I thought it was another opportunity to strike a few blows. I want to see a health insurance program passed. I've been interested in that since 1942 and I've only gotten to see Medicare, which is just a piecemeal part of it. And I would also like to see an improvement in the economic conditions of older people. I'm interested not just in the welfare of older people, because I think that so much of the welfare of older people is tied up with the welfare of younger people. One quick example is Social Security. Social Security is in trouble because there are a lot of young people unemployed who are not paying into the system. So our welfare and continued economic security is absolutely and directly dependent on the welfare of younger people. They should have jobs. That will not only help them but will help us, too. I'd like to see economic conditions improve. I'd like to see our housing program go ahead. These are the kinds of intermediate goals which can add up to making things a bit better than they are.

I've often pondered the contradictions of death and haven't found an explanation satisfactory to me. Here's one of the paradoxes. If wars had to be fought by old men, they wouldn't be fought. But a young man twenty years old, with fifty or sixty years left to live, will risk his life. An old man has only five or ten years at risk. Why is the young man more ready to risk his life, when he's risking his whole life, than the old man, who is only risking the ragged end of his life? The paradox is that as you get older your fear of death is softened. I've seen a number of my friends and associates die. I lost my wife. You start to see death as a natural part of life. You don't dread it and fear it the way a younger person does. I just can't understand this contradiction.

I have signed a paper, approved by my lawyer, that says if my doctors, by a determination approved by another doctor, say that there's no chance that I could ever live a normal life again, they're supposed to let me die. A lot of other people that I know have done that, too. We're only saying, in effect, let nature take its course. I don't happen to believe in reincarnation. I think that if there's such a thing as eternal life, then it's a matter of quality, not quantity. If one lives fully and meaningfully and richly, then the thought of endless continuance isn't particularly appealing. Let it be over.

Some people find, of course, a lot of meaning and sustenance, spiritual sustenance, in the idea that they are going to continue living after their personality or soul, whatever, leaves the human place. Cicero once wrote an essay concerning old age. In one of the passages he is talking to philosopher friends and says, "I prefer to believe that I will have an existence after this life because if I don't, none of my friends will be alive

Introducing a Brighter Shade of Gray

to say, 'I told you so.' If I am, I will be able to point at the skeptics and laugh at them.'' Kind of a nice thought.

I look at it this way. It doesn't bother me that I wasn't here in the year 1877. I was nonexistent. There was no part of me — body, personality or anything else. Why should it bother me that I won't be here in the year 2077? You came from nowhere and go back to nowhere. The period in between, whatever is allotted to me — the quality of that life is what's important.

Philadelphia, Pennsylvania

Maggie Kuhn—Age 72

I'm most like my grandmother, I think. Grandmother Kuhn was a spunky little piece — a little bit of a person with a lot of drive. Grandfather Kuhn, who had a farm near Buffalo, ran the last Underground Railroad station that smuggled slaves to Canada.

Father was largely self-taught. Poor, he had gone to work at fourteen. He taught himself Latin, some Greek and mathematics. Then, in the fashion of Horatio Alger, he worked up from office boy to district manager with Bradstreet, a credit agency (now Dun and Bradstreet Inc.).

Father was a liberal theologically, but just a stinker so far as his social and economic views were concerned. When Bradstreet moved Father to Memphis as district manager, he took on some of the prejudices of the South. But not my mother. She went back to Buffalo twice, to give birth to me in 1905 and to my younger brother, Sam, because she didn't want us to be born in the South. Mother was strong, but overprotective. She lived to be ninety-one, and my father lived to be eighty-six.

I guess in my old age I'm an extension of what I've been since adolescence. When I first tried as a young woman to be my own person, my father opposed what I was doing — the new and revolutionary thoughts that I was thinking, the people whom I was meeting. I was involved, luckily, in some of the early beginnings of the women's trade union movement and the organizing of young women who were working in very bad situations.

I suppose I was a rebel as a little girl, too. The day my brother was born, they tell me I ran away and they couldn't find me for several hours. And my mother's sister, who had been active in the suffrage movement, lived with us. She was a widow. Her husband had been killed in a train wreck, and she influenced my thinking and helped me to read. She read to me by the hour, and this was an opening.

The women in my family were strong, and they had to be, because men were autocratic and dictatorial. The women had to be this way in order to stay alive.

I graduated from Case-Western Reserve in 1926 with a degree in social work, and after that I worked with young girls at the Cleveland

Introducing a Brighter Shade of Gray

YWCA. I was appalled at the manners and values of the youngsters. They were second-generation Americans, living along the lakefronts. So I tried to superimpose my values on them at the YWCA. I tried to teach them etiquette at suppers. That was the standard way then, but I slowly realized that we were raising a generation of old maids who couldn't relate to the men around them.

This realization was a turning point in my career. My work in the YWCA became more radical. I began to do union organizing in the sweatshops of Cleveland. I worked with the YWCA for twenty years in Cleveland and Germantown, Philadelphia, and New York City as a publications editor on the national staff, and then in Boston with the General Alliance of Unitarian Women. I worked for over twenty years for social justice and peace as Associate Secretary in the United Presbyterian Office of Church in Society. Before I retired in 1970, I was Coordinator of Program in the United Presbyterian Division of Church and Race.

In the spring of 1970, shortly after I retired, I wrote a memo to five friends who were also working in various national religious and social service organizations. We came together to discuss a common problem — our retirement.

The Gray Panthers began with six of us sitting around a luncheon table. We met to see what we could do to use our new freedom in a responsible way. We all agreed that retired persons had freedom, experience and time to work for social change and engage in various kinds of social action. Also, that they needed opportunities to work together to reinforce their action. We met monthly, bringing other friends and colleagues along. Each meeting brought more people and greater enthusiasm. By the end of the first year, the group consisted of about fifty people. Today the national mailing list has grown to more than seven thousand people in all parts of the U.S. and in several foreign countries.

It was in 1971 that the name "Gray Panther" appeared first. The name was the idea of a New York City TV producer. I tell people that the "gray" stands for the universal fact that we are all, young and old, aging. "Panther" comes from the militant symbol of the Black Panthers. But my definition of militancy is not violence. It means devising strategy against age discrimination that will work for teenagers as well as people in their eighties and nineties. A Gray Panther is a person who is in general agreement with the Gray Panther's goals and principles, works with the organization and calls him or herself a Gray Panther.

We've attracted young people as well as old people because Ageism goes both ways — hurting both the young and old — depriving both groups of the right to control their own lives. We are striving to eliminate the great repressions society has built. I got involved because I have great concern for social justice. Old people and youngsters are discriminated against and repressed by society. We are both restricted in credit, income, housing and employment. And our nation's nondelivery health care system and lack of mass transit for the elderly are scandalous. We're not getting a fair shake, and I intend to right the wrongs.

Our society has largely succumbed to the Detroit Syndrome. Only the latest model is desirable. All kinds of pressures, including planned obsolescence, are applied to make us throw away the old model and get the new one. This has seeped into our thinking about people. Society tries to persuade us we are obsolete, that we are waste people just because we're not the latest model. We have been so completely brainwashed by society that we devalue experience and consider it no longer useful. During consciousness-raising remembrance we see, after all, what we have learned through the years has continued usefulness today, that there is a continuum of human experience.

Consciousness-raising among groups of us oldsters is basic to our own image and self-esteem. It is also basic to societal change and redirection. The larger goal of consciousness-raising is, of course, self-determination. We give lip service to being a democratic society, but by and large our lives are governed, managed and manipulated by forces beyond our control. The self-determination which we seek cannot be achieved unless the people affected by decisions are involved in making, enforcing and monitoring them.

I'm an activist. I don't sit back and say, "Oh well, that's life." I visit banks, corporations and transportation officials and remind them that there are older people with needs. I want to create an atmosphere where people can create themselves. Starry-eyed idealism isn't worth two hoots. You have to act, get tough. The trouble is that very few Americans are really action-oriented.

Arthritis was the first signal of my aging. It's a common affliction of age. Then I had to hold on to bannisters when going up and down stairs. About the same time came wrinkles. I do not regard wrinkles as hazards, but as badges of distinction. Oh, and my hair started falling out. Not all, just some. I'm proud of my gray hair, wrinkles and arthritis, and I intend to use them as credentials for a change. We can use our infirmities, our weaknesses and our deficits as an enormously powerful social weapon. The tendency is to say that we can't be active anymore. We can't take an active stand because we're sick. I say that's a cop-out. Our very weaknesses

Introducing a Brighter Shade of Gray

become our strengths, the lever for social change. We've got to stop feeling sorry for ourselves and stop depending on other people. I can't do all the things I did five or ten years ago, and I get furious about it. But I can find people who will join with me, and together we can do more than I did five or ten years ago because we've got each other.

Even sick people can be the instrument of social change. The medical profession is one of our targets. Those of us who are old are the largest consumers of health services and have a certain view of the health care system. Medicare pays not a dime for preventive health care, for the annual checkups that are so important for people of all ages, but particularly for people in advanced years. And how ridiculous to wait until we become ill and incapacitated before Medicare payments can be expended. Many of the doctors have scrap-piled us. They've given up on treating chronic illness. If we have arthritis, they tell us to take a little more aspirin and then they go away.

Health care should be handled the same way as public education or fire protection. School children don't hand over fees to schools, and you don't say to a fireman, "If you can give me a good price on putting out my fire, please come." We need a free national comprehensive long-term health care system for everybody. We already have socialized medicine in the armed forces. And the President and First Lady are the beneficiaries of socialized medicine. So if it is so great for the armed forces and Congress and the President and his family, we would like to have it for everybody!

Lack of mass transportation is a major cause of loneliness among older people who don't have or can't use a car. They must depend on a friend to drive them around, and one day they have no friends. Imagine it. You are lonely and trapped in your loneliness and helpless to do anything about it.

Legislators need to be aware of the clout we have. There ought to be old people on every planning commission and on every transportation authority. To bring the transportation plight of the elderly to government attention, volunteers who chauffeur old people around should stop the car pool and dump the people on the doorstep of the transportation authority. Until we get a place at the table, we must be highly visible. We have to come out of isolation and become the elders of the tribe.

One program we've started is called "Media Watch," in which our people monitor the news media for its Ageisms and complain to station managers if their news and shows project the wrong image. For example, we think that some commercials are a put-down. Old age on TV is seen as a disease — with death around the corner. The strength of old age, the vitality and wisdom of those who have survived, is not portrayed.

Older people are the fastest growing minority in this country. The networks should realize this. Their audience is no longer going to be comprised mainly of people who purchase layettes.

We're concerned about the gross neglect of people who are confined, really as inmates, in long-term care facilities. The medical profession has for the most part just walked away. They've extended life. They've made certain people into vegetables and then they've walked away from the wrecks and from any kind of moral, ethical or economic responsibility for the wreckage they've created.

Residents of nursing homes and patients have rights in this age of self-determination. And we who are on the outside have to be the monitors and the advocates, working with the patients' rights groups within institutions. But the residents themselves, the patients themselves, have rights that they must learn to affirm. We have put together the National Coalition for Nursing Home Reform, which includes citizen action groups in a number of states. We want to train people to be able to monitor services in nursing homes.

In Philadelphia's Germantown area, we are setting up cooperative movements to use the many big houses — the ones occupied by just one person — on a shared basis, either with other older people, or with younger couples. There is considerable interest among the elderly here to open up their homes to younger people rather than just sit in isolation in their own homes.

Unlike most other groups for the aged, we've stressed action from the beginning. Other groups are not action-oriented. They're too much like automobile and travel clubs and they offer no intellectual or social stimulation. The potential of some organizations is just not being utilized. Resources and talent are just being wasted.

We are a small group. We will never be a mass-membership organization like the American Association of Retired Persons. But in relation to our size, we have made a considerable impact. We are effective because we have created an awareness of our needs and goals, and we ask questions that need to be asked.

(Ms. Kuhn was not available for a personal interview but gave permission for the above selection of material from her speeches, writing and policy statements; some of the biographical information was excerpted from the WNET-New York TV broadcast, "A Wrinkled Radical," Copyright 1975 by Educational Broadcast Corporation.)

A Time for Doing

Whether or not adult life is truly a series of stages laden with predictable crises — a currently popular notion — remains questionable, but the question of retirement does not. It is a predictable, critical event in the lives of elderly Americans that affects both outer circumstance and inner feeling. Some of the impact from changes that alter lifestyle abruptly and dramatically, even though anticipated, can be shocking. A very obvious, immediate, and unwelcome one is the drop in income — which for the average retiree runs between 50 and 65 percent. And while it doesn't mean poverty for most, it doesn't exactly spell relief from financial distress either. It does mean a big change in shopping habits, an adjustment to a lower standard of living. One thinks several times about making purchases that were formerly made almost without thought. Ironically, some observers have interpreted the reduced spending of older people as a sign of how little the elderly need and that they have attained the simple lifestyle which is intrinsic to the wisdom of old age. The fact of the matter is that they just don't have money enough to buy more of what they want. This loss requires an adjustment, and we should not think it necessarily simple, since money — like sex — is a symbol of strength, self-sufficiency, and independence. Early morning brings awareness of another important change; for the alarm, if it goes off at all, no longer signals the start of old workday routines, which were probably followed for more than forty years. Any structure of such long duration undoubtedly provides solid supports for living, and the disappearance of this structure may breed insecurity. So retirement brings the classical identity questions: "Who am I; What should I do?" Whether recalled from earlier years, or totally unfamiliar, these questions at retirement frequently leap into mind with so bothersome an urgency that the new leisure can become a burden.

These are problems that impinge upon the newly retired, but they are not causing mass casualties. Studies show that most retirees adjust to their new situation and express themselves as satisified with it. Nevertheless, there is a body of opinion which recommends that older people should keep working for their own good. It cites the statistics that one-third of the retired population never wanted to leave their jobs and that there is a significant decline in health among those who suffer involuntary retirement. But most retirees do not look upon permanent work as a panacea. Those who were "stuck" at their jobs — workers in heavy assembly line industries especially — are pleased to be retired and would strongly resent any efforts to unretire them. Further, there are cases of retirees whose health improved after they left the daily treadmill. Undoubtedly, they are the ones who never whistled while they worked.

Although most retirees prefer receiving pensions to working for paychecks, there are those who, once off the job, flounder and cannot find a pleasing answer to "Who am I?" They tend to be former middle or top level management people whose job status had provided them with a good image of themselves. When everyone tells you you're important, the likelihood is you'll agree. Unfortunately, when so reassuring an occupation is gone, a good deal of distress may follow. And there are case histories of retirees from high status jobs who subsequently suffered deep depressions, acted inappropriately and regressed to extremely dependent behavior. The best thing for them would have been never to retire, but usually they had no choice. Another possibility, that of finding comparable jobs, was virtually impossible, since most American companies have compulsory retirement and others are reluctant to bypass their own personnel to hire older workers from the outside.

One way of avoiding, or at least reducing, the unexpected shocks that retirement may deliver is to prepare for them. The preretirement counseling programs that some colleges, private companies and unions have set up represent a good full ounce of prevention. People soon to be, and those already retired who attend them, find that exploring attitudes, expectations and future options with others in the same boat is a big help. Initially, it is comforting to know that a lot of other people are also getting wet in the troubled waters, which leads to the understanding that one's problems are societal in origin and not due to personal failure. Once having removed the guilt hooks from themselves, group members can be realistic — and thus hopeful — about the future. Then with their best energies, they can examine available options, make choices and start swimming.

The map that each elderly person takes away should correspond to the real land that retirees must walk upon. So while the former cohorts of big business will understand how slim their chances are to wheel and deal again, they will also know about opportunities for related experience. They can do volunteer work at private, nonprofit, social service institutions, where their organizational skills and managerial experience will be put to good use and be appreciated — excellent for self-esteem deficiency.

A Time For Doing

Not only former members of the managerial class need to have their sense of feeling useful restored. Possessing it is at least as important as income to every older person's well being. Nor is it so difficult to obtain. Any older person willing and able to venture a short distance from home base will find a host of opportunities.

The human-helping agencies, whose budgets are always too limited to meet the virtually limitless needs of society's neediest, such as the physically handicapped, the mentally retarded, disadvantaged children and the frail elderly—are always in need of volunteers. Public schools in many cities around the country are actively recruiting elderly volunteers as special teachers. The reward for helping those in need is an immediate sense that one is useful. It would be better for the elderly, in more ways than one, to be paid for being useful; younger people are, and money always helps. Nevertheless, for those whose retirement seems a dull drift from TV set to shopping center with possible golf and cards in between, the involvement may be more important than money. The time spent on behalf of others can transform the rest of the day into a brighter time and should even improve one's golf score.

Should anyone have difficulty finding a place to volunteer, contacting a local office of ACTION, the federal government's agency for volunteer programs, will provide locations both here and abroad. Remember the President's mother?

Living out a dream, which was sustained over the years by the hope of "when I have enough time" may also provide the elderly person with a sense that retirement is worthwhile rather than empty. No longer obligated by work, the retiree hears opportunity's loud knock, which over the years had been restricted to leisure time. But, ironically, when all one's time is free, the dream often ends up a disappointment. Something changes when a leisure activity becomes the sum of one's day rather than the pleasurable break from work that it used to be, and much of the pleasure fades—an experience not unlike what may happen to anyone on an extended vacation. However, if doing what one wants to do is respected, valued by, and of use to others, such as teaching a skill or being part of a theater group, then leisure activity goes beyond diversion or distraction. It becomes a lively, meaningful and pleasurable connection to the real world, which can establish retirement as the time of one's life.

Santa Barbara, California

Tom McKenna—Age 71

When I was about to retire I wasn't worried in the least. I looked forward to it. I didn't think of what I was going to do, not really. But whenever I saw an airplane fly over I would stop and look. Flying's something that I wanted to do all my life. I missed it extremely. I really love it. There was no money in aviation, and I had to make a living. There is money now — you should see all I put in it. So when I retired as a builder about five years ago — I'll be seventy next birthday — I had time on my hands. The first thing I thought of was that flying was a heck of a lot better than spending time sitting in the bars watching TV. I bought myself a 1972 plane. It's a fabric job with tandem seating and it's tail-wheeled instead of nose-wheeled. I fly about twenty hours a month approximately, and I just get a bang out of it. As soon as I finish anything, I almost always head right out to the airport and spend my time out there. People come around. I give rides over the city all the time.

I first started flying in 1928. I soloed in Camden, New Jersey, in 1928 and then before World War II, operated from a cow pasture in Wilmington, Delaware. I did barnstorming way back in the early days. I used to fly over New Jersey. I would fly over a field, and if it looked like I could land on it, I would fly back over the little town and goose my motor to make it sound like a forced landing, and then I'd go out and land, and everybody would come over to see the forced landing. Then I would take out a little brush and paint with white paint on the fuselage, "Rides $1.00, Acrobatics Double." I used to come home with thirty to forty-five dollars. Sometimes you would get permission to land on somebody's farm and do it all day. Then in 1940 I taught combat flying for the Army. That type of flying is no more, it's just history. I'm an experienced flyer, but I always find a lot to learn.

I give lessons now; I specialize in acrobatics — stunt flying. I don't charge for giving lessons, just for renting the plane. I usually start them out with spins and loops and Immelmans, slow rolls, Cuban 8's, square loops, and so forth. Most of the guys out there are private or commercial pilots, and they've never had a spin. They like relaxation when they're flying, so they come to me and learn some acrobatics, see what it's all about. Some of them, including some of the girls, like it so well they take an eight- or five-hour course with me. I had one little girl here, weighed about ninety pounds soaking wet, one of the best acrobatic pilots I ever saw. She'd say, "I want an hour of acrobatics." When the hour was up, I would say it was time to go in and she'd say, "Look, I want to do a couple of more spins."

I like acrobatics best. I still get a bang out of soloing with someone who has never flown a tail dragon. It usually takes anywhere from an hour or two to five hours for them to solo. It gives me pleasure when I take these kids up for acrobatics and they say, "Hey, man, take me out."

Sunday a week ago, I gave about four acrobatic lessons. For a young guy, two and a half to three strictly acrobatics is considered enough for a day. So some days, maybe the next day, I won't give any, and then the following day I'll give two or three. I give about twenty lessons a month. And I keep up with innovations. It keeps one on the ball, especially if they're going to do cross-country flying. I don't particularly care about doing cross-country anymore. I prefer sport flying, which is mostly local, hardly over fifty miles. Occasionally, I get some students who want to do low flying over the water, about five feet over the ocean. I may take a job towing gliders at Saint Inez airport — which will also include my acrobatic instructions. I'll be towing gliders, probably, mostly weekends. There should be eight days in a week for all the things I have to do. I'm going to have to do something about this.

Some of the old people think that there's no more life in them, that they're not capable, but I don't think they try. I don't think they want to try. They think that it's the end of the road for them; they've had their day, and they're supposed to sit back and let the young ones go ahead. I won't let the young ones get ahead of me.

We had to go over to the airport about a year ago. Dr. Haller's wife was with me and a couple of the other guys. We had rented an automobile, and the car gave us trouble. We were stopped on this big steep mountain, and we had to walk about five miles. Well, I was ahead of everyone of them until we got to where we were going. I said, they're not going to look back and say, "Hey Tom, come on." I was looking back at them, saying, "Hey, come on. What's the matter with you guys."

I get along with the younger flyers fabulously, absolutely one hundred percent fabulously. You would never know there was any age difference. It surprises me. When they have a little get-together or party or somebody celebrates a new rating, whatever the case may be, I'm invited to the party. When they're going up for a ride and they're alone and have an empty seat

A Time For Doing

they'll say, "Hey Tom, come on." Of course, I do the same for them. I'm known as the Old Barnstormer.

Occasionally, I go with somebody or somebody will go with me to an air show. After we register, they have free beers for the pilots; after 6:00, there's a free dinner. We sleep under the wing of the airplane all night. We get up the next morning, have breakfast, stay and watch the show and then go home. It's just like old times, sleeping under the wing of the airplane. It brings back memories. I happened to fly formation with the great Frank Tallman* coming back from the airport a while back. He's making a picture near Santa Barbara and flew under a bridge over there. I taught Frank to fly; I was his first flight instructor; I gave him his first job as a flight instructor in 1938. Frank flew in the picture, *The Great Waldo Pepper,* and in *Baa, Baa Blacksheep.* He's the owner of Movieland of the Air in Southern California. I had a good two-hour chat with him over old times.

My wife is not too much in favor of my doing all this flying. I find that's pretty much the same with the guys and gals that fly out there. Usually the gal's husband frowns on it, and vice versa. Pretty much standard practice. I wouldn't say it's dangerous, if one just uses common sense. Anything can be dangerous. Driving down the highway, driving all over the road and trying to get closer to another driver can be dangerous, the same way with flying. You inspect your aircraft before you take off each time, see that you have sufficient gas and know your capabilities.

I can do acrobatics that I don't recommend my students do. I won't do some things unless I do them alone or have someone who's flown a lot who knows. The law says you have to have completed a stunt at over 1,500 feet. I usually start them out at 4,000 feet, not close to the ground. I do all my flying over Lake Cachuma. I've been extremely lucky; I've never, never had an accident of any kind. I guess there are those who have and those who will, but I'll wait until that date. I've had some close ones. Once I was recovering from a spin and someone passed me about a hundred yards away. The same week I was flying down to Burbank — another guy was driving — and we both looked out and saw a 727 pass us at about two hundred yards.

Thank God, I have my health. The third of the month, I just passed my medical examination for second-class certificate, which we have to have. A commercial pilot has to have an examination every year, a private pilot every two years. Anyway I passed my test in August and the doctor said, "Tom, I don't know what the hell you're doing, but don't stop." So I'm good for another year.

*Frank Tallman died in May 1978 when his plane crashed in an attempt to land during a storm.

It would be nice to take a survey about the differences of attitude between old people and young people. James Arness said a couple of weeks ago that he wanted me to give him a couple of lessons in my airplane. I said, "Come over any time." He said he would take the lessons, but he was too big to get into my airplane.

I keep my weight down. I've got to, because I couldn't get in that little airplane if I don't. I weigh 175. I take physical exercise every morning when I get up. I do a little jogging and I watch my food. I eat a small salad for lunch. I eat a good dinner, and if I see my weight going up, then I cut down a little more. I feel perfectly healthy, and have no problems at all.

I wish I had never had to work. I wish I could have done nothing but this all my life. I look forward to continuing as I am. As long as I can pass my physical. My bird is the only one of its kind in the field. In fact, there's only one other acrobatic plane. I don't worry about not being able to fly, not really, but I say to these guys, "Hey, when I get old, will you take me for a ride?" They say, "Hell man, you'll be flying when we can't." That's a good description. I never cease to appreciate the beautiful view. Retirement's definitely a happier period for me. In other words, I'm just starting to live the second half of my life.

Chicago, Illinois

Ed Rawson—Age 76

I was a reluctant person, not wanting to become involved in different things. In December 1975, I had just become seventy-six and retired from Monsanto Chemicals. My wife and I were celebrating our fiftieth wedding anniversary with a big trip to Hawaii. Suddenly my youngest daughter, who knows Patrick Henry and the Free Street Theatre, said, "Mom and Dad, you've got to come down and see what these people are doing. They're going to start a senior company and they're looking for people to join." I had known about the junior company, attended their performances a number of times and admired what they were doing with Patrick Henry. Our reaction was, "Forget it, we're going on this trip. There's no time." But our daughter persisted. She told us the Theatre had received funding for a one month program to develop a senior citizens' theatre group. "You better join. It'll change your life," she said.

My daughter has some great ideas about cultural activities, about what older people should do, and about the theatre in general. I argued with her. I told her that I had never done anything like this in my whole life. I had never acted, not even in school. I told her, "Your mother has been an accompanist and has a lot of stage experience in school and acting, but forget me. I can't do it. Besides, we're going on this trip."

Well, she took us down there on a cold January day in 1976. I wanted to meet Patrick Henry and tell him that I couldn't become involved. If there was an opportunity to work with children, okay. I'm great at working with kids. When my children were growing up, I improvised with them and told them stories I made up. I did the same thing with my grandchildren and all my nieces and nephews.

That first day about twenty young people were there with Patrick Henry. A lovely young lady came up to me and said, "I'm going to interview you." So I spent all day in a room with her and a tape recorder. She said, "We just want to know your life story." And I said, "Okay, I'll start at the beginning." I told her my earliest memories. I didn't pull any punches either; I told her everything, both good and bad.

The interview went on for two days. On the third or fourth day, others appeared. We began to mingle, have group sessions and talk. I didn't really know what was happening. For a week we improvised, performed skits and studied mime. But I was still very puzzled.

One day we were sitting around talking, and suddenly Patrick Henry said, "Ed! I want you to tell some of your stories." I was reluctant, but I did, and everyone was fascinated. I talked for a half-hour, and they said my stories were the most delightful things they had ever heard. When I got through telling them, Patrick said, "When you hear Ed tell a story, you get goose pimples."

I always could tell stories, but I shied away from telling them in public. Even though occassionally I would get wound up and people would become interested, I had a tendency to be shy, just a good listener. I began to see that I really did have a creative talent, but I was suppressing it. This project did something tremendous for me. I found that I didn't have to be shy socially. I could have done more and been more outgoing.

This triggered something else. After a couple of weeks, I realized that in my working career my strengths had always been my imagination and mental ability. In fact, I was always inventing the whole time I was working, and eventually had about thirty patents. I never got any money from them. The value of these patents to me lay in developing something from scratch. I designed them, tested them, and made improvements. I even had something to do with their manufacturing and sales.

The first couple of weeks with the group I was very skeptical. I thought the idea wouldn't go anywhere. I didn't understand what was going on, and I never thought they could keep seven people together as they have. I'm amazed that we did stay together, and it's all due to Patrick Henry. He's quite a guy.

He's trying to bring theatre to those people who have no opportunity to see theatre. He's trying to say something important to people. In our case, his message comes via strong individual stories. It's oral history. He's trying to join intergenerational activities and break away from the stereotype of age. And he's struggling for funding. We participated in the productions on a voluntary basis until August of last year. We didn't go into it for the money, but Patrick Henry insisted he wanted to pay us. I think that was smart. We received funding for a year, and it held us together. When a salary is paid, the task becomes a job and a responsibility, and people won't say, "Next week I won't be available." If there's a dropout here, it's serious. Ours is not like a conventional play; there are no backups, no understudies. Our production is so personal it's not easy to find someone else to step in. We expect to persevere, and we hope to get more funding. We're going to Milwaukee on Wednesday, to the Pabst Theatre. We're going back to Ann Arbor, Chevy Chase. They're booking now. Those trips will be made on a voluntary basis. We get our expenses paid, but receive no salary. That's all right — we're not in it for the money.

I think we've become very professional. There's a confidence we possess, a feeling that we're doing something well. We actually get professional comments on it. The last performance we gave was at a college here. NBC came in with a full video crew and filmed it. They wanted a five-minute piece to televise on a news show, but they ended up filming the whole production. The director has experience and is a pro. He said, "That was a powerful thing, and professional, too."

The very first performance was horrible. Up to the last minute people were changing scripts like a troupe of amateurs. I was getting scared. Patrick Henry finally realized that we would just have to work without a script. Some we memorized, while the rest was read from scripts in our hands. The idea was so good that CBS decided to do a documentary on us. During the whole month while we were developing our theatre, their crew was here, filming everything including the first performance. The film was trimmed to a one-hour documentary that appeared on prime-time television last June. It won three awards. The documentary includes some clips from the performance. Whenever I see the acting we were doing then, I cringe. It was horrible, and a far cry from what we're doing now.

Of course, there are days when you feel close to the audience, almost as though you're talking to them. Other days you have to force yourself to communicate. You might expect that repeating a show would become boring, but it isn't. Each show is different, because we're in different situations, in different places, with a different audience. Every show is interesting to me, and I feel proud doing it.

I've had this attitude throughout my working career. No matter what I did, I always took pride in my work, and I think that's the key to satisfaction. When I was sixty-six, I went to work with Monsanto, a big chemical corporation. They didn't know I was sixty-six. I looked pretty young for my age, so I told them I was fifty-seven. I could have told them I was even younger but it was too hard to fake the resumé below fifty-seven. Monsanto just didn't check very thoroughly. It's hard to get a job even at fifty-seven, but they saw something in my resumé they liked, so they hired me. I handed my thirteen patents to them and stepped down to a lower level.

After working there seven years, another company took over Monsanto and began revamping. I was hired as a consultant, but I lost all my benefits, so they increased my salary as compensation. I stayed on for another five years. When I was seventy-six the company contemplated moving to Saint Louis because business was falling off. But the Saint Louis office was becoming edgy about me, since they had a company policy of retiring people at sixty-five. They told the Chicago office they would have too let me go soon.

Seventy-six is the age to begin relaxing, so I retired and they gave me a big party. I planned to continue consulting, to take a few trips and to take it easy. Then the theatre project came along. It keeps me very busy. During the months of June and July we must have done at least thirty-five performances. It has become practically a full-time endeavor now and I'm sure it will step up again.

If this had been a theatre group strictly for seniors, with no young people involved, I don't think I would have stayed with it. I'm a little different from the average older person. I'm not a joiner. In most of my activities, I'm a loner. One of the reasons that I'm a loner is that it's hard to find someone my age who can keep up physically.

Take bike-riding. I've been riding for many years, and not just ordinary bike-riding: I ride with professional equipment over long distances. It's no trick for me to go out and ride twenty-five miles. I usually average fifteen to twenty miles when I'm riding every day.

I used to play golf, too, but in the last ten years my regular foursome died off. I became depressed about it and I didn't want to break in with new people. I have friends, but none of them are athletically inclined.

It's important for me to stay active, involved and, I hope, healthy. I don't want to go the nursing home route. I've had a lot of contact with nursing homes. My father was in a nursing home, and we've had friends in all types of nursing homes. I had the same depressed feeling every time I went to one. I said, "This is not for me!"

The biggest reservations I had about joining this theatre group with seniors was from a health standpoint. But look at what has happened. We ended up with seven people whose ages range from sixty-five to seventy-eight mostly, and in the year-and-a-half we've been working, we've performed about seventy-five times. We travel around, do a lot of rehearsing and generally hard work. And do you know, we have not missed one performance — not one!

A Time For Doing

We also have workshops and other activities in addition to our regular rehearsals and performances. Robert Joffrey of the ballet comes here every year. He's a friend of Patrick Henry. Once they needed a lot of extras for *Petrouchka,* so Bob Joffrey called Patrick Henry and said he would like to have some seniors sent over. We all went and did four performances. I thought we would just be a bunch of dummies, but no, we had to work a lot and learn our parts. I got a terrific bang out of it.

Technically, we're called the "Free Street Too," because the junior company is called the Free Street Theatre. We fell in love with the young company and they with us. They're a wonderful group of people. It's funny. I find that I have a much closer feeling with the younger people than I do with the seniors, the people I'm acting with. I like the seniors, but when it comes to socializing, we're more friendly with the young people than the old people. Why? I don't know why. The older group is fine and we get along well, but I guess I just really enjoy working with young people.

A lot of times, both with students and senior citizens, the audience sees seven vital people on stage, and they think we're special people. We try to tell them we're not. We have discussions after performances, when we sit back and try to get their responses, without our talking too much. When I do talk, I tell them that there are lots of older people out there who would be eager to do the same thing.

Doing theatre work is changing me, and that's something I get a kick out of, too. People notice the change. They've never seen me talking so much before. They've noticed my laughter, and my wife is laughing, too. You see, you're never too old to learn. I get a lot of fun out of acting, even knowing I'm not going to be a great actor. I've grown in terms of actual technique. I had never done anything like this before, but now I have confidence. I know what I want to do, and I do it.

Fond du Lac, Wisconsin

Ethel Rucks—Age 77

When I first came back to Fond du Lac after my husband died, I wanted to work, but I didn't know what I wanted to do. I tried sales. This job with handicapped children came accidentally through my nephew, who was working as city administrator. He asked me to assist with an aide system at one of our schools. I didn't know what to expect. It was very different from anything I had ever known. The school administrator said, "How do you feel about it?" I said, "Let me have a go at this for nothing for two weeks." Now I've been working at the day care for almost eleven years. The center is independent; that means we are not supported by town, state or federal funds. We had just one paid person, and that was me. Later we began a bus system, which we had to pay for, but the rest of the workers are all parents and friends who volunteer their help and raise the money through fairs, fund drives and card parties.

I've always cared about the underdog, the handicapped. And being semi-handicapped myself—I don't raise my right arm—I've never felt a strain working with the handicapped. I've felt for them. We have a boy who has gone blind. He is so ambitious to do things; he's so happy to hold a brush in his hand and move it over to the paint cup. I feel so sorry for him. But they don't want sympathy. You must never show that. I don't let them feel that I notice the difference, that they're handicapped. You just have to play down their mistakes and realize they're handicapped rather than obtuse, and they all have some one thing they do better than we do.

If you hurt their feelings, they cry. I don't ignore that. If I inadvertently hurt their feelings, or someone else has, I treat them like children. I take them aside and talk to them. The biggest satisfaction is to finish the day without any crying. I consider it a very bad day if anyone cries in the afternoon. Every one of them is very highly emotional. We have Mongoloids. And one is brain-injured and doesn't talk. Two are blind; one has been blind since birth, and one as a result of spinal meningitis. He's in the hospital more than he's out. He's a singer.

When I took the job, they said all you needed was to be twenty-one, have patience and tolerance. Tolerance is important. And you really have to believe that those people can do what you expect them to do—and

A Time For Doing

always—that they're lovable. That's the main thing—they want a little love and attention.

I think the older person can be more understanding because older people often feel handicapped by age; they move more slowly, don't see clearly and sometimes are slow to answer a question. I have one young man, an epileptic. You have to have patience with him when you ask him a question. If someone says, "Hurry up," he freezes. I don't think that a younger person who hasn't had any experience at all with age would understand that. It's empathy.

We try with academic things, though we know they don't have much academic interest. Their interest span is so short, maybe ten minutes. And each is an individual. Music is our strong point. They do very well with the harmonicas. They did very well with everything on the Christmas program. There's one boy I feel could become a soloist.

I've thought a great deal about changes I'd like to see made in the care of the handicapped. Last Friday I was the first to receive the Wisconsin Easter Seal Society's Most Concerned Citizen's Award. As I told them in my thank-you speech, I would like people in every walk of life, when they see a handicapped person—in a wheelchair, blind, deaf or crippled—to recognize that person as a brother or a sister or a neighbor, rather than to comment, "Oh, she's blind," or "Oh, she's crippled." "Why is she in that wheelchair?" And never to talk down to them.

We need volunteers with our crafts and ceramics. The students love ceramics, and they love to paint; they do a good job. There are some people who can't do this job. Some of our volunteers can't do it. I say, "Don't feel too badly. Probably I can't do some things that you can do. Just do something else." We had one parent who would do anything—but she can't come out here and help us. She can't face it.

I'm going to retire in a few weeks. I'll miss them. I decided to retire because I felt that I wasn't producing as much, and there are a few things I want to do that I haven't had time for. I thought the students should enjoy some of the younger people, and we got one to take my place. She's forty years younger than I; at seventy-seven I can't be as active as I was.

When I was eight years old my home was broken up because of my mother's death. I spent time with a wonderful family, educated people. Maybe that had something to do with my attitude toward anybody who is handicapped in body or in mind.

Ethel Rucks

I always did do something outside my home after my children were of age. At one time I was supervisor of a cafeteria. My interest in life has always been people, wherever we were, or whatever I was doing. My vision of the world has broadened. I would never have known about the handicapped had I not gotten this job. I've discovered their problems, and what can be done to help. You learn so much by doing.

I would have liked to have gone to school more than I did. I intend to take courses this winter. I don't know which ones, but they'll be for enjoyment; certainly not just for credit. I believe in and am interested in church work and all the things it involves. I haven't been able to do as much as I'd like because of my job, but I want to help more in the church now.

My children like the work I've done. They think I've achieved a lot. One of them never knew till last Friday that I was getting the award. He was quite surprised. He'd never been in the building where I work. But the other two have, and my daughter always stops by whenever she comes through.

I've got a lovely family, three children and fifteen grandchildren. One of my children has two children, another has four, and one son has nine. He's the teacher of the family. And three of his children are also teachers. Two more are in college, and they also intend to teach.

My older son is quite busy right now. I see my daughter more often; she's the closest. The other son comes whenever he can. And of course I visit them. There is no lack of family contact. We always get together in summer, at Christmas, whenever we can. I want to spend more time with my grandchildren; the youngest is three, the eldest is twenty-seven. One is at Connecticut University. Another at West Point.

For pleasure I drive, read, and I love to crochet. I don't watch television much. I play a game of cards occasionally. I like to travel as much as I can, and I'm getting a little more travel in now. I've never been East and I want to go. I was born in the western part of Wisconsin and I've been there most of my life. According to my children, I should get out and visit some of the places I've always wanted to see.

I'm not afraid of dying. If you do each day what you think you should, you should not be afraid to die. I don't say I want to die; there are many things I want to do. But if I die suddenly, well, I've had a life I liked, with nothing to regret; and even though some of it was a hard life, it was also very good. I had a loving husband and three good children.

San Antonio, Texas

James MacKay—Age 86

Saint Louis was my hometown. I taught in Saint Louis for twenty-six years, until 1946. Then the Veterans Administration borrowed me and I was sent to the University of Arizona to set up a VA guidance center. While I was on a leave of absence, Trinity University in San Antonio heard about my work and offered me the job of turning their VA guidance center into a public one. It was the first time I had worked outside of public education. After a year with them I joined one of the local schools as director of guidance.

I retired in 1959 when I was sixty-eight. Mine wasn't a mandatory retirement. My boss even asked me, "Why are you retiring? Nobody's pushing you." I told him there were some things I wanted to do.

Mrs. MacKay and I went to Europe. At that time the dollar was worth so much more and as long as we traveled second class, we could stay as long as we pleased. We stayed for thirteen months, just bumming around, going where we pleased. When I called the office of the World Federation of Mental Health, of which I'd been a charter member, they said they could use me. The office arranged for me to lead seminars in every country I visited, and it set up lectures for the parent education commission because I was a child psychologist. I had been director of guidance for the public school system and guidance counselor for family problems. That had always been my work.

When we came home from Europe, I began to study gerontology. Since beginning my studies, I have received more honors in gerontology than I ever received in my life's work, mainly because I entered the field on the crest of the wave. I read that about fifty to ninety percent of the people placed in mental hospitals after the age of sixty-five should not be there. They have simply become too cantankerous and their families can't handle them. I went out to the hospitals to see the people, and they agreed with that estimate. That sent me to work on determining why the elderly become unmanageable. I joined every organization for the elderly I could find — the group in my church, the AARP, and the Council on Senior Citizens.

I concluded that these people lacked meaningful activity. A group of us asked the city council to establish an office of coordinator of senior activity. In our community there were quite a few things going on, but nobody knew of them. The city council accepted our suggestion.

Texas is divided into several councils of government. San Antonio is the headquarters of one which comprises thirteen counties. It's a big territory, and San Antonio is its only large city. The local council of government was asked by the Governor's Committee on Aging to establish an office on aging. When they did, I was elected to be president of the task force that organized it. By the time we finished setting up the office, my term as chairman had expired, but they asked me to stay on as a volunteer staff member. I'm still registered as the consultant on gerontology to the Administration of Aging here. I have spoken before the legislature on insurance problems of the elderly. Last spring I appeared before a congressional committee on counseling of the elderly.

Currently, my major activity is establishing peer counseling projects; it's a pilot program for the state. I have training and research classes in which each month I train a group of older people to help other older people. After the fifteen-hour training course the class meets once a month. Each group may have as few as seven or as many as thirty members. Within the last five months, we've trained about seventy-five to eighty people. We have only half that number actually working with us, but we have many people coming in to be counseled. We are now training people to work from community centers. We hope to continue this for the next year. After the initial training, we have a monthly meeting of all the counselors for in-service training. I'm handling the research.

I'm also involved with the Institute of Lifetime Learning. We have become so big that we enrolled over 3,500 students last year. We are in need of funds because we have to go out on the open market to get teachers. When the Institute was small, our teachers were virtually volunteers, receiving only expense money. I am working on a project with the Office of Education and Office on Aging in Washington. They have combined recently and I hope to become involved with them. Although I'm no longer the director of the Institute, I do teach my classes. I teach a class on the "Sands of Time," in which the students outline an autobiography. We really have a ball. I'm able to stimulate memories which people haven't recalled for years. In the spring I teach a course called "The Psychology of Happiness."

Happiness is so dependent on the individual that I can only give a general formula on how to be happy. I tell my students that basically they are responsible for their own situations. I have a couple of guidelines. One, it isn't their actions but their reactions that count. Two, they must learn to face reality without allowing those realities to depress them.

People should enjoy the pleasures of the senses. That sounds bad to old people because of the Puritan ethic, but as we get older, we lose our senses of hearing and sight. Those who have lost their senses of taste and smell are subject to malnutrition, because everything tastes like hay to them. Many older people won't cook for themselves because living alone makes cooking inconvenient.

I teach them that the sense of touch is the language of love. When our grandchildren are too old to be cuddled, and we don't have any great-grandchildren, we should hold hands with old people. Contact is very important.

There's the joy of association. Some people like a crowd, while others like a one-to-one association. People are very different, but man is gregarious. We should recognize this and not shrink from meeting people.

There's the satisfaction of service, which stems from feeling useful, not useless. For me, the positive part of old age is continuing to help people. I teach people not to grow old, because "old" connotes obsolescence and uselessness. But these are generalizations.

We're each so very different. Older people have the same individual differences they had as children. In addition each of them has led a very individual, distinct life. You can't discuss old people as a group, although there is a tendency to do that. The only thing we have in common is that we have lived a long time. People will say, "He's eighty years old. What can you expect?" When I hear people talking about an eighty-year-old man, I tell them I'm eighty-six. They're pretty surprised.

There are basic differences in working with kids and with older people. One, children are inexperienced and you have to guide them and help them get experience. Elderly people have this tremendous background of skill and knowledge and wisdom that you must get them to use, but which society does not encourage them to use. Two, all guidance for the young is towards the future. Our guidance for elderly people is toward adjusting to the present. Our senior years are dynamic. We are changing. We retire at the height of our power. Eventually — at eighty-five, ninety — you're going to be dependent because you're going to die in bed. It's just as dynamic as childhood, but it's the reverse — you're approaching dependence instead of independence. An older person knows what he's doing, but a child doesn't know where he's going.

James MacKay

I haven't encountered prejudices against my age. I heard myself referred to as a legend and felt as though I had been placed on a shelf. Then I established a new career. Some years ago, my two sons thought I shouldn't drive my wife out West, a distance of 2,700 miles. I said, "Why, is there something about my driving that's worrying you?" It was just on general principles, they said. I soon popped that one—I drove out there. We fly now, because I don't know if I could drive for such a long time.

My biggest satisfaction may be the deference I receive. I just love it. Young people know that sitting in a straight chair is pretty hard for me, and they'll look everywhere for an armchair. When a young person gets up on a bus and offers me his seat, I thank him and take it. I'm proud of my age. I think that the deference I receive and the fact that my young cousins write to me and discuss their problems with me give me the greatest satisfaction of all.

My family life's been wonderful. Some of my grandchildren write to me with questions they wouldn't ask their parents. I have cousins from the third and fourth generation now that save their problems until "Cousin Jim" comes.

We have a very close family. I have a seventeen-year-old grandson who's staying with us now because he wasn't doing too well as a senior in high school. I was talking to him the other day about doing his work ahead of time instead of letting it go until the last minute. It's like putting money in the bank and being able to spend it when he wants to. He said, "Grandad, you know, you've got a point there, but you seem to have a point every time I talk to you." My son, daughter-in-law and wife don't think I'm so bright. They bring me their problems, but they don't like my answers because I toss their problems back at them.

I tell my classes I like to teach because as teacher I get a chance to talk. I have had so much fun in every field I've pursued that I can't say which I liked best. I must be two hundred years old to have had all this fun.

I've gotten a few honors along the way. I was selected Senior Citizen of the Month by the NCSC last April, and I was very proud to find my name in the *Who's Who, American Men of Science* in recognition of my work, even though most of my work has been on a person-to-person basis. I've written a few books, the latest dealing with retirement, but never had any published. It takes time to find a publisher, and I'm just too busy with other things. The same is true of my painting, which I started at seventy-nine. I could sell these paintings if I had the time to follow the art shows, but I give them away to make room for more. The only problem is that I like to give them away in frames, and they cost about twenty dollars.

A Time For Doing

To stay fit, I swim and I work two or three hours in the garden in the Texas sun. I have always been physically active — swimming, tennis, hiking. I was a scout leader for twenty-three years. My garden and swimming are my main activities. I have my aches and pains and take pills for them. The old carcass does have weak spots now.

My most difficult situation is to see my wife failing, but there's nothing I can do about it. If she came to me for help, I could help her. I think she's doing marvelously, but she thinks I'm kidding her. We've been married for fifty-eight years and it's hard to take. My wife just broke her hip. I was visiting her in the hospital, running the house and taking care of my outside commitments. The work load became too heavy and I realized I had encountered a limitation.

I think I can face reality better now that I have learned to analyze situations and use my wisdom. As I told one of my sons, I've finally learned that I have limitations; I've realized them and faced them.

Still on the Job

Except for a small group of exceptionally wealthy people, the one common experience of most Americans is working. For some people, work is a burden, unpleasant, and just the way to get by. For others, work is the source of great fulfillment, satisfaction and even identity. Many times, the first question asked a new acquaintance after his name is, "What do you do?" Lots of older people would prefer their usual answer, but cannot give it. About eleven percent of those over sixty-five are still at work, many of them at the jobs they have been doing for their entire adult lives, while others, no longer on the job, wish they were.

There are a variety of reasons for this desire. When retired people were asked what they missed about working, the first thing they mentioned was income. But equally important was the lack of daily contact with their work buddies. Almost three-quarters of the people questioned by the Harris organization in 1974 so responded.

This points out one of the significant pleasures of working and, in fact, of being alive — the joy and comfort that comes from being with others. In a work situation, it's there aplenty. Even when it's not all fun: the missing raise, the mean boss, an unwanted assignment, or office intrigue, the camaraderie helps. For people without families, especially, but also for those with an active family life, co-workers are part of an extended family of sorts, and the place of work is sort of a home away from home, where one spends a big chunk of the day.

More than sixty percent of the interviewed people said they missed the work itself — the feeling of being useful and having things happen around them. This feeling, too, is a human necessity. People need stimulation, must have things to anticipate, to look forward to, and to feel that what they're doing has meaning. As self-contained and self-generative as one may be, it is difficult to create that kind of environment alone.

By now, everyone knows that there is an unwritten policy, an aspect

Still on the Job

of Ageism, among employers on hiring older people. One-third of people over sixty-five would like to work, but can't find jobs. Those in the position of hiring confess that there is descrimination against older people. Paradoxically, the Age Discrimination in Employment Act is for young people and doesn't protect the rights of those over sixty-five. It's no wonder that the elderly don't feel wanted by business — they aren't.

Which is not to say that the majority of older persons want to work indefinitely. They don't. But those who do are denied the choice by mandatory retirement. And that denial is a violation of freedom that no other age group in our society endures.

Aside from these emotional letdowns, retirement, particularly forced retirement, can bring on health problems. Among men, common illnesses increase dramatically. The American Medical Association in 1972 wrote of a direct link between unemployment and bad health: when a person has nothing to do, an overconcern for the body develops and there is a tendency to exaggerate the most minor physical and emotional symptoms. Probably the most frightening evidence for this is the death rate of those men who retired involuntarily. Their average life expectancy is twenty months. It's literally true, then, that it is deadly for a person who wants to work to stop.

Forced retirement is one of the major problems for the elderly in America today. It is a dreaded fact of life that has caused distress to one-third of the present retirees. Given a choice, they would have chosen to continue working. The recent federal law did not eliminate compulsory retirement, it merely postponed the axe dropping at the age of sixty-five to seventy. Elderly workers are still waiting for liberation for a law that will enable them to work as long as they wish and are physically able to do so.

According to another Harris Poll conducted recently, seventy percent of people under thirty-five were in favor of extending the age of retirement. They did not buy the idea that a person's age is all that determines his or her ability to do a job. Ironically, one of the common arguments presented by advocates of complete retirement is that there won't be any jobs for young people, and the business world will be stymied by a population of old, obsolete workers. The obvious untruthfulness of that latter notion aside, if the majority of young people, who will supposedly be so adversely affected by the law, do not feel threatened, why the fuss?

Many people continue to run their own businesses after they turn sixty-five or seventy and many professionals maintain their usual office hours. Neither customers, nor clients nor patients have complained. While people at sixty-five cannot be expected to have the same stamina as twenty-year-olds, their physical changes certainly don't mean the end of usefulness. Proof, the thousands of retired elderly people who find new careers: a salesman becomes a writer; a housewife finds she has a talent for working with the handicapped; a physicist suddenly becomes stagestruck; an office worker is accepted for on-the-job training in a Social Service agency.

Another form of encouragement is that the attitudes of business towards the elderly do seem to be loosening a bit. Some in management are acknowledging the great wealth of experience and competency in the population over sixty-five. Employers are becoming aware that experience and maturity are as desirable as youthful zip. They have discovered for themselves what studies reveal: older workers are more punctual, have less absenteeism, are more careful than their younger counterparts. In Illinois, a local bank was having difficulty with the young people in its clerical division. They were careless and the large margin of error in their work was causing headaches. The bank's vice-president hired a sixty-five-year-old woman to fill one of those positions, and much to his delight, found her error rate to be practically zero. Now the entire unit is comprised of unretired people over sixty-five. This is only one example. U. S. Steel is another. It has more than 1,000 workers over sixty-five on the payroll. And those who may be physically unable to continue at their old jobs are transferred to ones they can manage. That's enlightened policy. Although the attitudes of employers are not exactly reborn, business is hiring elderly people and patting itself on the back because the results prove that it's good business.

Those elderly who are at the jobs they have been recently trained for, or which they have been working on for years, have the same feelings about their work as younger people. While some do them only to make sure that the bills get paid, others love what they do; it's their whole life and their passion. The satisfactions that were there thirty years ago are still there, and new ones come along all the time. Their work is central to their lives; their pleasure from work is inestimable, and old age in no way diminishes the capacity to feel such gratification.

If national legislation is passed, if state governments continue to modify their own retirement policies, if the attitudes of employers keep changing, it will not mean that people will be forced to work when they want to retire. But for those people who wish to stay on their jobs, and continue to earn a living or do what they love, no single birthday will be an ominous stop sign. The options allowed younger people will also be available to the elderly. Instead of a population that feels marginal and unwanted by business, America's older people can become an integral part of the country's economic life, which should benefit not only both parties, but the entire nation as well.

New York, New York

Herman Langsner—Age 75

I never thought of leaving dental technician work. I've been in the field since 1914, so that's sixty-three years. When I graduated from elementary school, my father wanted me to learn a trade, and so he sent me to a dental lab. My father was a butcher and had a customer who was a laboratory owner. This customer seemed to like me, and he said he'd teach me his trade. You know, the old foreign folks wanted their children to have a trade. I wanted to go to high school, but my father apprenticed me to this man, and I was getting two and a half dollars a week running errands and picking up work and bringing it to the laboratory.

It was quite ridiculous how much time I wasted getting work. This laboratory was at 115th Street and Second Avenue, and I had to go to Knickerbocker and Hart Avenue in Brooklyn. I still remember that address. It was hard for me as a youngster to find that street way out in Brooklyn. When I left the lab at nine o'clock I took my lunch, because it took me five or six hours to go out there and back. The charge at that time was fifty cents for a repair job.

After that, I was learning. The thing that intrigued me was when my employer opened his drawer. He had so many instruments and tools and pliers, spatulas, scissors and little hammers — so many instruments that I said to myself, "My God, do I have to learn all those instruments in order to do the work? I will never be able to do that." I watched to see how people did things. Once I felt that I knew a little, I left that place, went to another laboratory and told them that I could do the work. Naturally, when I went to do it, I was a little slow. When the boss remarked on it, I said that I was nervous from being at a new place, and that when I got acclimated I'd be faster. Soon I was gaining speed. I worked in a lot of labs and never got fired; I always quit to advance myself.

I've worked in a lot of labs. I have been the head man, but I never bossed anyone. When the messenger came over and talked to me, I listened. You don't know how many ideas you can get from listening to these youngsters who ask why you do a certain thing. Other people would chase them away; I never did that. Unfortunately people in this industry feel that if you don't do things their way, you're wrong. I tell my students that their

Still on the Job

boss might not approve of my methods. I tell them, "If he disapproves, do it his way. You will find out later on which way is better."

A lot of the youngsters that I worked with are now running their own labs. They're my competitors today and still have good things to say about me. I feel I have accomplished something.

We're really prosthetic dentists when we put teeth into people's mouths — the same as these fellows who make arms and legs for crippled people. A dentist usually makes the preparation for the bridge, and then he sends it to the lab, and that's where the technician begins. The science is when you get it, work it out, plan it out. It's engineering, too — all these things you have to *plan* out. What is medicine for one is poison for the next. I can do a job for one person a certain way, and the next time the same patient can't tolerate it the old way.

I'm still learning, but as for innovations or new techniques in the field, I don't know whether I can improve. When you get older, what do you mean by improving? You see, there are new techniques; and I'm getting so that I'm staying with my old techniques. But I feel that everything new today we did years ago. They've come out with a new atttachment. Well, that's not new to me; I saw that fifty years ago. To these youngsters, it's new; but it's nothing. In fact, for certain teeth that are bell-shaped, I always had the idea that the crown does not have to go under the gum of these teeth. I always used to advocate that, but the dentists didn't want it because the patients didn't want it.

It's creative work; when I make a set of dentures, I feel I'm really creating something. There was a time when I made a bridge that looked so good I didn't want to deliver it. I love my work. There are evenings when I can come home and take a piece of Ivory soap and carve myself a tooth. I do a lot of carving.

I've been giving lectures since 1938, and now I teach three days a week at the Educational Alliance Settlement House. I enjoy my teaching, and I'll tell you why: by teaching, I'm learning. I'm truthful to my students. I don't beat about the bush. I just tell them point-blank I'm not God; I don't know everything. I say, "I'm going to show how I do it. If you do the things that I do in a different way, and it comes out the same way, you're right, because it means that it's easier for you to manipulate it that way."

I still run my own laboratory, but because I teach three days a week, I'm two days away from my lab and I have to work to catch up. I would like to learn how to speak Spanish so I could speak to my students. I read books on it, but I don't know the pronunciation. You need a teacher for that.

I went to high school and to NYU at night. But I really don't have time to, now. Besides my lab and teaching, I go to lodge meetings. I have to attend the dental lab owner's association. I have a wife who likes to go out occasionally. I have a son who just graduated from medical school; I like to go to baseball games with him. I'm a member of the Museum of Natural History. I give clinics, too. This is the fourth year I have given a clinic in tooth anatomy and tooth carving for the New York Laboratory Guild.

I haven't considered retiring. I enjoy my work. What will I do if I retire? What is there to retire for? I don't know of any other technicians my age. They just fade away. But I don't. I don't think my experience makes me unique in my field; I don't flatter myself. I respect everybody's ability.

But I like life. I'm not a wealthy man. I have to work hard for things; but still, it doesn't discourage me. I got a letter from my granddaughter; I had sent her a check for her birthday. Well, here's a sixteen-year-old worrying about getting older. At my age, I worry about—will I be here tomorrow? Life is a worry all through, from the day you were born; it just is something you have to expect.

An old man like me . . . you know, the will is there, but the body isn't. I'd like to go out and play some baseball, but since I was mugged, I've got an Achilles tendon. Now I limp a little bit; I can't walk like I used to; I always liked to walk. The doctor told me, "Herman, act your age." I still like to do things a youngster does. Until I had the accident, I used to coach a Little League team. I had one hundred and eighty kids, from 8:00 in the morning to 5:00 in the evening, Saturday and Sunday.

I like getting up in the morning to see what life has to offer me. It's like gambling; you bet on something and you wonder what's going to happen, or like taking a card and hoping you're going to get the right one; that's all life is. I enjoy my life. I have no regrets. It didn't have to be nightclubs and fancy restaurants. The things I've done make me feel like I've accomplished something.

Baltimore, Maryland

Todd Duncan—Age 74

I always knew that what I did would have to be in music. That's when I'm happy, healthy. I've been blind to anything else. Next to performing, I love teaching young people. The rewards are different. I get joy and fulfillment from teaching. It's satisfying to see the students accomplishing things, it gives you a sense of why you're here in this world. When I hear a student with a wonderful voice, I have only one idea: to make that voice even better. I know so much more than they do and I have so much to give them. Students study with me from four to five years. I teach graduates from conservatories — New England Conservatory, Eastman, Juilliard.

I have so many demands on me and I have never said no. Though I am learning to. I teach as many as forty students a week. I have my own studio, and I have students who come to me from all over the world. They are semiprofessionals who sing opera, lieder, French songs. I am a master teacher at Curtis Institute in Philadelphia. I have a beautiful relationship with my students. I look forward to doing what I am doing — developing young talent. Bad health is the only thing that would make me give up teaching. I'd like to die with my boots on.

I've gone from concert stage to opera, to Hollywood to recordings. I've sung for royalty and at the White House, and that was exciting. It's hard to say what I'm proudest of.

I retired as a performer when I was sixty-five, but I have performed since, usually an operatic role with a symphony orchestra. I had mixed feelings when I retired. I'm outgoing and a ham by nature; I missed the audiences and everything that goes along with it; meeting people. But then planes, trains and hotel rooms are very tiring. I did an average of one hundred and fifty concerts a year. I'd be in Europe from August until December. I'd come home for Christmas, and right after Christmas I'd leave again for South America.

When I retired I knew there would be an amount of sadness that would come to me, but that if I used my mind instead of my heart I could accept it. No, I never feel a sense of envy, but I did sometimes when I was younger, when I heard a great baritone.

I have a sense of humility and fulfillment. I created the role of Porgy forty-one years ago. I did a one-night singing stand in New York the year before *Porgy and Bess* opened. I got rave reviews from all nine New York papers. George Gershwin heard about it. He called and I went to audition. I sang just half on an Italian song when he said, "Will you do Porgy?" I was very naïve then. I thought of Tin Pan Alley, so I said, "I don't know. I'll have to hear your music first."

The advice I give my students is: Know what you want and want it hard enough, and what seems like hard work to others won't be hard for you. You may have the talent but you've got to work. When you get tired practicing and practicing, then you've just started.

I think your treasure is what your love is. A person is what his values are. I believe that in the creative arts there is another level of the emotional and the spiritual, and that level doesn't know any age. Sometimes I get up in the morning and I don't feel like teaching, but when I start nothing hurts anymore because I'm in the spiritual world, the creative world. Those of us in the creative world might have something that goes along with longevity.

A great desire and need started me singing opera, a gut, visceral desire. At that time there were no Negro opera singers, so I studied all the black roles in opera.

It makes me happy that a Negro doesn't have to do that nowadays. I was the first Negro to sing opera in New York. I've trained for the opera all my life. I started studying piano with my mother when I was five years old. I started studying voice when I was seventeen; I did Porgy when I was thirty-two, and that whole time I had been studying. I had nothing but encouragement from my family.

I would love to have been at the Met. It wasn't the time. I don't think I'm bitter about it but I'm quite aware that my beloved country did not give me that opportunity, or anybody of my race then. Other than that, I have no regrets. I did feel frustrated at times, but I never felt that I couldn't do it. Racial prejudice was frustrating. There were many concert halls where I couldn't sing. And I wouldn't sing in segregated concert halls, or halls in the South where Negroes couldn't come to hear me sing. There were many social pressures. That's better now. Roland Hayes, Marian Anderson, Paul Robeson. They helped.

Paul Robeson had a difficult time of it. I myself wouldn't have done what he did — go to Communist Russia. We had many sympathetic conversations but we disagreed vehemently. Once he said, "Todd, you're selling your race down the road." I felt I was on the stage to sing. I didn't use it as a platform. This man was brilliant, but we just didn't agree on this thing. Every man has his view of politics, whether he works on the railroad

Still on the Job

tracks, at the White House or on the concert stage. The artist is not oblivious to this; but I question whether an artist should use his success and position this way. It takes so long for an artist to prepare himself that I question whether enough time is left for him to know the issues. I have the right to my ideas, but to use the concert stage to put forth those ideas — I don't know if I have that right.

There's an increase in interest in opera. Little opera companies are springing up all over America. But the concert field is not what it used to be. Rock 'n roll is taking over. I tire of rock 'n roll easily. There's just a beat to it, an animal beat, no depth, nothing intellectual. After the first bars of the first song, it's enough. There is a kind of music with beautiful lyrics, very thoughtful and philosophical — what kind of music do you call it? — I like that. I was never a part of the counterculture of the sixties so I never felt left out of it.

I'm glad to see President Carter interested in the arts, willing to fund them the way they do in Europe. I think there is a greater interest in the arts here than in Europe, though I wouldn't have said that thirty years ago. What is real and honest and moving has no boundaries, not political nor racial nor linguistic.

Growing older, I think I am a simpler man. I have a beautiful home, I'm looking out at a thousand sailboats. There's something about nature that's wonderful, and I think I have a greater appreciation for it. In my earlier years I was more ambitious for the almighty dollar. That is farther from my mind. My understanding of what I want to say through my singing has probably changed over the years. I cannot stand intellectually, emotionally, spiritually indifferent performances. Any change in me has been a change in depth.

I've had a very good life, a happy life. I've not been neglected, I've had a lot of love. A wife, a son, a grandson. I have no fear of death. My one fear is to linger like a vegetable. But I have no fear of passing on to another life. My son and I are very close. He's gone to Dartmouth, Harvard, was Phi Beta Kappa, is a corporation counsel and Dean of the Harvard Law School. A very brilliant guy. It's so true that children of artists often get short-ended, but he's turned out wonderfully.

San Francisco, California

Walter Stack—Age 70

I moved to the Bay area in '37. I was in Canada for a few years but I was on the East Coast before that. I'm from Detroit, but I went to sea from New York and the Gulf. Then I came out here by land. I went to Seattle on a thing I was asked to handle for the strike committee of the Seaman's Union.

I quit going to sea in '51. I was a victim of McCarthyism, being accused of being a left-winger and I got eased out of the industry. After some odd-and-end jobs I went to a slaughter house for four years as a knocker. The knocker beats the animals to death with a hammer. I left the industry a year before the humane slaughter law was passed. One day I was killing a bull and I threw my back out; I ruined my back. I had to make a living, so I looked around for all kinds of work. I had a job driving a pickup for a couple of months. I worked managing a liquor store for six or eight weeks. It didn't pay too well.

I was about fifty years old when I started working as a hod carrier. It's a strong construction union on the West Coast, but I knew a business agent, a drinking buddy, and I asked him if he could get me some work. A month later I asked if he could get me into the union and he said sure. The work was so hard I thought I wouldn't last, but I got used to it in two weeks.

A hod carrier is a kind of helper to a bricklayer or plasterer. He mixes the material, goes up the scaffold. It's a grueling job. Nowadays things are carried up hydraulically, but hod carrier remains the name, just as teamster is the name given truckdrivers, though they no longer drive a team.

There's no mandatory retirement where I work, but if you can't handle it you get fired. Most people when they get to sixty-five are happy to get out. There may be one or two others around who are sixty-five or more.

Work is the curse of the working class. I have a sense of pride, so I'll do the job, but I've never been proud about doing the job. If you owned the machinery or the plant, it would be different. You know the boss can only advance at the expense of the worker, and the worker can only advance at the expense of the boss. There's a basic contradiction.

I'm relatively casual about the money thing, working. I've always

Still on the Job

been militant, with a progressive social standpoint. I've been a Communist for forty-eight years and I've been victimized so many times as a result of that I just take everything in my stride. I don't get excited about anything. You can be thrown off a job; I figure this job is good while it lasts — three weeks, eight months. I don't give a damn. It kind of breaks my heart to go back to work. Except I need the money.

I feel I am treated with dignity. I wouldn't associate with people who didn't treat me with dignity. Oh, there's a big difference from the way I was treated at forty-five. As you get in my age category, people have a tendency to be more respectful. I was pushing a wheelbarrow along and there was a superintendent about forty-five who called me "Pop," and said, "Let me give you a hand, there." People want to show you that they have respect for age. If supervisors have something to say, they'll couch it in careful terms. What can be a pain on the job is an obnoxious boss, or anything that insults your dignity.

My name is always good on the job. I'm not resented for keeping the job of a younger man. I pay my dues, they know that; if I want to work four or five months a year, they understand that, too. It isn't that I enjoy working. It's the check that counts. But I like this work. I find this interesting.

But I can't think of anybody on the job I've socialized with outside, going to each others' houses, exchanging dinner invitations. Not even drinking. I drink at home. I have about four or five drinks before supper. Who is a friend? I belong to a club made up of my running buddies; we get together for dinners and that sort of thing every two weeks or so. I'm involved in organizational work and I enjoy putting in the hours. It's a real pleasure; you know you're doing good. There are a lot of parties connected with the runners — most people who run are professionals, white-collar workers, relatively affluent. Few are manual workers. I'm invited to more parties than I can handle. Rare cases when there's anyone there my age. They're younger, but we get along fine.

I wasn't athletic as a kid. I got started biking, hiking. Later, when I was a seaman I used to swim ashore from the docked ship. And when I wasn't working, I'd go swimming. I'd swim two miles in the morning. I joined a club that swam under the Golden Gate. I swam to Alcatraz. I was fifty-five when I started that. I started running at fifty-eight. I thought running would strengthen my swimming. I organized a running department in our club and organized three other running clubs.

My first distance was a mile and a quarter, and I kept doubling it every

Walter Stack

three to six months. I've been running seventeen miles a day for six or eight years. Once I hurt my ankle; another time I had to wear a neck brace, but I didn't let it stop me. I started getting up earlier and earlier to run, sometimes at 2:30 in the morning. I'd run seventeen miles, swim, bike, shower, sauna, so I could be on the job at 7:45. I had to give up running or sleeping, so I cut the running down. When I'm not working, I get up at 5:00; when I'm working I get up at 2:30. I'm too tired to run after working. If I can't get a minimum of five hours sleep I won't do all that exercise the next day. It's easy to do, getting up early, you just make up your mind you're going to do it.

Road running has become the center of my life. Running and swimming give me real pleasure and satisfaction in life. I've been in all the magazines and on TV programs, through these sports. All this attention is not because I'm doing things sensational in themselves, but because someone of my age is doing them.

I'm in top condition for my age; I never bothered checking with my doctor before I started running or swimming. I have a very low pulse rate. My heart is excellent. I've been given stress tests all over the country. I'm a good man for stamina. I just had a stress test with a stamina-testing machine, pushing a weight back. They said try to do it thirty times; well, I did it sixty-five times, and they were astounded. I beat everybody who had ever done that test, including the youngsters. That surprised me.

I love running, cycling. I make some money in competition running. Secondly, I'm involved in building trades, I'm very socially conscious. I want to contribute to the advancement of labor. But the amount of good I'm doing is relatively limited, so next year I may retire.

When I was younger, my goal was advancing social change. Only forty-five or fifty years ago I'd give hours, nights, days. I'd be fanatically concerned when I believed in things. Now I feel my time is more limited. Now I don't know that I have a goal. I have a bunch of short-range goals. Each race is a goal, setting myself a certain number of miles, speed or distance.

I'm toying with retiring. But once you do that, you feel you may be severing connections, especially when you've been involved in something for so long. Some people have talked to me about a job promoting physical fitness. But if I retire, I want to take it easy. I'm not sure what taking it easy means, but I think it means not getting myself into pressure situations.

Being older doesn't bother me a bit. My wife is sixty-five; that's kind of a problem. She minds getting old, but that's society's pressure. I notice

63

Still on the Job

one thing. Most older people tend to favor the status quo; they look back on the good old days. There's a tendency to become more set in your ways and become intolerant. I say you've got to resist this. It's all right to have contempt for some specific thing, like vandalism, but to develop racial or social bigotry isn't good.

Talking about dying doesn't bother me. I decided to will my cadaver to the medical school. If I can give my eyes to help someone, why not? When I'm dead, I won't care. The ideal way to face death is in the saddle. Or running, that would be best. I don't like the idea of becoming senile. My wife and I don't discuss death a great deal, just once in a while. There's no immortality. Everything is subject to change. Ideas, too.

Laguna Hills, California

Ruth McFadden—Age 76

I've only been in this career eight years. I decided to work because I enjoyed it. I do estate sales. I don't sell real estate, but price people's possessions and sell them.

I haven't been a working woman all my life. But I worked on Wall Street until I was married in 1928. After I was married I worked for charity and had a Girl Scout troop, that sort of thing. Then for ten years while both girls were in college I had a job. Between the time I was sixty-five until sixty-seven I just kept house and worked for the election board. I was in a women's club. One year I was president. They were all retired and I had to train them. We had a local history group, and we had a group that studied antiques. The club itself met once a month. The special groups met once a month. I was never bored.

I arrived at Leisure World thirteen years ago. We were living in Los Angeles. The neighborhood was changing and we decided to look for a retirement place. We decided this was it. We could go into L.A. within the hour. Our kids were in L.A. We thought it was a good buy. This was the best decision we ever made. I have a manor. I have two bedrooms, a bath and a half, a patio.

My husband died in 1968. I've been widowed for nine years. I'm seventy-six now and lost him when I was sixty-eight. I'm not the kind that sits around and moans. My life did not change drastically when my husband died. But I will say that I'm glad we moved here before he died, because I made a lot of friends that helped me out. I could easily have been lonely.

I'm in a community where the residents are fifty-two or over. The average age is sixty. We've been running about thirteen years, so there are plenty of people here over seventy. We have some ninety and one hundred. There are about thirteen thousand people here. They have sold their homes and come here to Leisure World. Some of them might have had ten-, twelve-, fourteen-room houses, and now they're here in two bedrooms and a living room. Everyone owns his place.

I settle estates and sell for people who are moving from their places in Leisure World, where they have maintained themselves, to total care facilities. It's like living in a hotel. And I sell when people die and their heirs want to get rid of things. A lot of people live here whose children live in New York or Chicago. They don't have the time to stay on and take care of liquidating. I get twenty percent commission.

I've been doing this for eight and a half years. I did antiques for a while. I had CPA training. I worked for attorneys. Very often when I liquidate an estate, I have to satisfy the courts with prices that I put on things. A friend of mine died, and the attorney who handled the estate was also a friend of mine. That's how I got started. At first I had to be careful how much I worked, because I was getting Social Security. I went to town after I got to be seventy-two. One year I made $10,000, another around $8,000. I have a pretty good reputation. I'm working because I enjoy it and I want to leave something for my children.

As for a typical day, well today was an easy one. I'm up at 6:30. I did patients' mail today in the hospital; I have eight girls working under me, all volunteers. There's a lot of bookwork. I got out of there at 1:30. Then I came home, sold two or three things to people, I paid off some people and gave them their checks. The people are in the house sometimes while I do the sale. A lot of times there's an agreement between me and the executor to finish the sale before the place is sold. There's a lot of screening of the people who are coming to buy out the place. Then I went over to help a lady who can't really cope anymore, went over her checking statement and settled up her account. That took two hours. After that I came and waited for a woman who was moving here from Florida to sell her some furniture.

On an 8:00 to 8:00 day I may sell things to a lot of women. I will have to go back at 7:00 in the evening when their husbands come and sell *them* the things all over again. Sometimes I'm on the go from 7:45 to 8:30 at night. I'm worn out after a day like that. I just want to come home, get a book and go to bed. I have a little drink. After a day like today, I feel fine.

The part of the work I like the best is the pay. I like to accomplish something. When I do the way I should, it makes me feel on top of things. It's a little bit hard to say how much work I'm doing for pay. I work by appointment only. As a result, I often run several sales at the same time. Sometimes they run for two weeks. Sometimes I make deliveries. I'll be at one place from 10:00 to 2:00 and another from 3:00 to 5:00. Each day is different. Some days I have a little time off, but I do something practically every day. Some weeks I take in about $2,000 to $3,000. I have had quite a bit of experience marking prices, so sometimes I help some of the others out with that. Usually antique things.

Besides work, I enjoy traveling, swimming. I've been to Hawaii and

I'm planning to go to Mexico. I have a lot of energy. I always did. Last night we went out to dinner. I enjoy going out to parties. We have an evening in the park almost every weekend. Most of them I don't enjoy because I work all day. I belong to local history clubs, which I enjoy. I also belong to a sorority which I joined in my days at New York University.

Here at Leisure World we have organ concerts, bridge clubs, the opera, and there are all kinds of other clubs. So you just have no reason to be lonely. I used to do horseback riding. I do swim every time I get the chance, usually daily. I don't play golf anymore. I'm a little arthritic, like everyone else.

I'm much freer now than when I was younger. Much more my own boss. I never could have carried on the work that I do now if I still had my husband. Now I'm absolutely an individual person. I've never had these satisfactions before. My husband was the ruler of the household. These last few years have given me satisfactions I never had before. I've earned my money and I can spend it for trips and things. And for my house. My daughters and I have a ski cabin in the mountains which I never would have been able to have before. I have quite a bit of pride. I give them useful presents. I like to give and not just take from them.

I don't have any problems that I didn't have when I was younger. I still worry about money. I do a lot of thinking about it so that my estate won't be eaten up by taxes. I'd take a pill before I'd use it all up. Life is more relaxed for me now. My husband was a worry-wart. We had the children to worry about. Now I only have myself.

I borrow other people's problems. I worry about my grandchildren. I want my girls to do the right things. I still am concerned, although they tell me to relax. I've been involved with my grandchildren their whole lives. They come down and work with me. They all pitch in and go to the sales and work hard.

My husband was a retired engineer. Besides Social Security, I have his pension and other income. I didn't have to work, but I decided to in order to leave the amount I had to my kids. I got into business and I love it. I have three grandchildren and I would like to see them have good educations. With the price of education what it is, the money I'm earning will come in handy. I don't spend as much time with them as I would like, but we have a very good rapport. One daughter lives in Las Vegas. She teaches there. I see my children about three or four times a week and then sometimes once every few months. I put in around a thousand miles a month driving around.

Still on the Job

I'm ready for death any day it comes. I put in one of those living wills and have it signed. I don't want to leave too much of a mess. I don't want to linger and I want them to let me go. I don't care to live forever. I've had a full life. I've enjoyed my life. I'm not in the least bit afraid to die. I have done enough in my life and I will never die as long as my children and my grandchildren are concerned. I'm gone—so what? The things I've taught them will live on. It's important for me to know that my children and grandchildren will remember my principles. Honesty. To help the other person. That's my immortality.

New York, New York

Vera Lachman—Age 73

The trouble with me is that I'm addicted to teaching. The whole situation, to love a subject and then transmit to someone who is eager to get it, is very very sacred to me. It's an affirmative human interaction. "I want to know something. You know something about it. Please tell me about it." That makes sense to me and I seem to be cut out to do it.

I have been teaching two mornings at the NYU School of Continuing Education for four years. I teach two mornings at Brooklyn College in the pilot program for equal opportunity students, which is made up almost entirely of black students. I teach a class at NYU in Classical Studies, a two-hour Plato Symposium. I teach one course for the New School in Intermediate German and another in Beginning Greek. Two students at the NYU University Without Walls asked me to be their advisor, and I also teach them. This is a program which ends in a master's degree. Then there are really private lessons that I give in my home. I'm teaching fifteen hours a week this semester. That's a normal load for professors of any age. I find it a bit tiring, but I would rather do too much than too little.

I had been teaching at Brooklyn College for twenty-seven years before my retirement, which was mandatory. I had mixed feelings about retiring, mostly regret. I thought, "Now I can travel. I can go to my place in North Carolina when the violets bloom. I can see the turning of the leaves. I can sleep till all hours. I can go to museums." I was retired for ten days which I enjoyed greatly. Then a former student of mine came to tea and asked how I felt about my retirement. I said, "Partly wonderful. Partly blue." She said, "Would you like to teach a class at NYU?" I said, "Oh yes!" She asked to use my phone, and two hours later I was given a course to teach. That was four years ago.

My favorite subject is Greek. I started reading Greek and Latin when I was a child, and I decided when I was eleven that teaching would be my life's occupation. I had a rather famous cousin who was in the first generation of women to take their doctorate at the German universities. She happened to be a classicist. Both my older sister and I heard her lecture and knew her, and that was an incentive. My sister started taking some Greek first, and when I heard her reading out loud from the first verse of *Antigone,* I made up my mind, and I went to my mother and said, "This is what I'm going to do. That's final." She took that seriously and encouraged me. Greek is an addiction, basically. I teach Comparative Literature which is natural; I had to learn so many languages. My PhD. is in Icelandic. But I do not teach these other subjects with the same enthusiasm that I teach Greek.

I came to America on a nonquota visa in December 1939 as a refugee, and I was admitted through a contract with Vassar College to teach German. The first year was very hard. There was terrible academic unemployment, and I was just one of an army of refugees flooding the market. I worked as a cleaning woman, a dairy worker, a lowly library worker and all sorts of other menial jobs. At first I had mostly substitute teaching jobs in colleges and private schools. I finally joined the City University of New York system, teaching full time.

Aside from the high unemployment and the fact that I was thirty-five, and that was considered not so young, I had one great handicap. I couldn't speak English. I had studied it before my immigration, but only briefly. I took a book that I liked very much, Lawrence's *Seven Pillars of Wisdom,* and I put an English version and a German version side by side. I was trying to learn through a bilingual method. It only worked a little. When I came here, I was lost. I thought, "I want to have one benefit from this terrible immigration. I want to read Shakespeare in the original." It took me a year to read the complete works. I began to speak that kind of English. When I came into the department room at Vassar I would say, "Methinks it will be eight o'clock. How fare thee today?" They laughed at me, but it was so much easier than modern English. I couldn't even read the newspaper.

I had never really taught in Germany. I took my doctorate in 1932 from the University of Berlin. You had to take a so-called state exam, which was really a preparation to teach at a German university. I couldn't take it at first because there was still a great animosity towards women teaching, and then Hitler came. I started a school with some friends for students who had been discriminated against. For six years we taught children; Jewish ones, or children who were half-Jewish and half-not, and who were therefore not acceptable to the traditional schools. After six years the school was closed by the government. I came here a year later. So I have been very grateful to be able to teach. I haven't made great efforts, but the gods have been kind.

This class that I'm teaching now at Brooklyn College is an entirely new experience for me. These young people have had no opportunities, and sometimes it's a little bit more like social work than teaching. The challenge to open up to them a new world is just something I like. I'm delighted because the class is going so well. There are three or four whom I haven't reached, but the others are looking forward and asking lots of questions. At first they were annoyed and said, "What is this all to me, and what are these names, and what do I have to do with it?" One Jamaican woman said to me, "I want to train in computer science. Why do I have to take a class in Homer?" I said, "You don't have to. Talk to your advisor. It's very possible that you can get out of it." She is a devotee by now. She sits in the first row and eats it all up.

Of course, this seduction act is part of the teaching experience. I enjoy that part greatly. If I feel there is no contact with a student, I first go through my circus tricks. If it doesn't work, I try to shove that student into another section or find him another teacher. I cannot deal with it and never could. I just arrogantly expect that everybody will be very glad to be taught by me. It's like I'm a Pied Piper playing my music and seducing people.

I think my students think I'm a crazy old woman — oversentimental, always emotional. "She knows a lot. Her tests are too hard. Her assignments are too big. She's a little ridiculous, but she is better than some of those boring teachers. We have to help her along." They rather patronize me. In general, they become fascinated with what I'm teaching. I was voted favorite teacher of the graduating class of Brooklyn College a few years ago.

There's much more difficulty with the faculty. I have had a long record of getting into trouble with my heads of departments and my immediate supervisors. They find me very hard to take. "Opinionated," one of them wrote. I don't fill out lists well and I won't hand in exams on time. I don't budget my time in the correct fashion and I give voluntary office hours. This has caused me to be criticized often. When I was younger, my supervisors didn't like me. I wasn't easy to manage. I was stubborn and I wasn't very cooperative. As you get older, they get used to you and find you a necessary fixture. You give the department a bit of color, so they put up with you.

When I'm not teaching I write poetry. I have published two volumes of poetry, and my poems have also appeared in magazines and newspapers. I don't set aside a special time to write. These things are inspired. I am totally passive. I wait. Then, splish, it comes out. It comes out very fast and often surprises me. I write in German, and I have a translator with whom I've been working for twelve years. When I do a reading on the radio or in public, he reads the English, then I read the German.

I used to go horseback riding for sheer indulgence. I can't do that anymore, but I still enjoy myself immensely. From movies to eating, I'm very sensuous. I enjoy our little home here. I enjoy people, children, the outdoors and life in general. I also paint sometimes — little watercolors of cats, flowers and landscapes. I don't paint with any claim to great art, but just to enjoy it.

I have very little to say about death. I had a severe heart attack two years ago, and although I was saved, it was the razor's edge. You remain conscious and say to yourself, "This is it." The greatest regret is leaving all the unwritten poems. That was my first thought. Also, I love some people very much and I don't want to leave them. When one gets old, one loses one's friends. They go ahead and graduate from life, you might say. It's very painful. Throughout my life I have lost those who were very dear to me, so death has always been with me. It's not just a development of old age. Last summer I lost a cat who had been with me for sixteen years and seemed like an extension of me. I miss him terribly. All my reasoning—cats die, he didn't have to suffer—didn't help. I empathized with him. As he became weaker and weaker, did not eat or drink and became more mixed up, he knew somehow in his animal wisdom that death was coming. I was very much that cat.

I am looking forward to doing the same things I have always done. The highlights in my life are my trips to Greece and going to my summer home. Also, since my last book was published, I have about twenty-three new poems. You need about fifty for a book, and I hope that I will be given more poems. That is very important. I am still changing my teaching methods. I would be dying of boredom if I didn't. I'm not a scholarly writer. What I have in the way of new insights I put into teaching. It's one way of transmitting my new thoughts on old things to other people. Sometimes even new thoughts on new things. As long as I am halfway in good shape, I want to teach, and teaching keeps me in good shape. I get so warmed up and happy when it's been going well, I know it's something that I will never give up.

Back to School

A mingling of gray with ivy green is becoming more fashionable on college campuses these days, as older people accept the invitations to learning now being extended by the educational establishment. Quite different a generation ago, when this was virtually unheard of and an older person could be compelled to drop out of school because of administrative indifference and faculty and student hostility. Although the campus may still have some barren places for an older student, the grass is generally greener today.

The new look is partially the result of improved societal attitudes and partially because the colleges are in trouble and struggling to keep their doors open. Like many businesses, the schools need customers, that is students, but they've been running out of them. The postwar babes, those born during the nation's last big fertility boom, have all graduated and in the process left too many empty classrooms behind them. A brief study of demographic charts indicates that there will not be enough younger brothers, sisters, and cousins coming along as replacements; however, each year will see an increase in the number of leisure-time grandparents looking for something to do.

Opening the ivory towers to the elderly seemed a logical move for the college administrators and the socially responsible as well. Another influence on the new policy was a political push from the state legislatures. Within the last six years, twenty-four of them have mandated that their state-financed universities make higher education accessible to the elderly by offering them much reduced tuition fees. (At the University of Minnesota, this has translated into a two-dollar per credit bargain rate.) For gerontologists, the prospect of intergenerational campuses is pleasing. It evokes the unique image of serious meetings between the young and old that could have a ripple effect through society, stimulating desirable changes.

Back to School

It's difficult not to view the implications of higher education for the elderly as the promise of a warm spring. College is the place we send our young to get the tools which will enable them to dig up sufficient knowledge and understanding of how to do and be well in the wide world. For the elderly to participate in that experience would mean that they were unraveling a psychical knot, declaring themselves ready and able to grow stronger. It would be an expression of confidence in their own capacities, for since attending college involves competing against the competent, computer-generation young, it represents a threat. Approximately 10,000 elderly at schools around the country, who are fully matriculated students aiming for a degree, have had the temerity to join the regular college crowd and try their strength. That's a very small percentage of the total college population and even less of the elderly's, which proves that the idea of going back to school does not send older people eagerly racing to the registrar's office. There are however, other nonmatriculating elderly persons on the campuses, attending classes and taking courses made available to them at one out of every three colleges in the country. But after that fact, the promise of an intellectual spring becomes vague. There is no data on who is offering what to whom and to how many. No one knows how many elderly people are going to college or receiving instruction from college faculty on off-campus sites. Furthermore, concerned educationists are very critical of what they consider a casual attitude toward the elderly at many institutions where fun and games have become the extent of the education being offered. "Beginning Macrame" and "Advanced Bridge" have a place in an older person's life, but if nothing else of more intellectual substance is in the course catalogue, then the schools seem to be operating on negative assumptions about the elderly, assumptions inappropriate to institutions of higher learning. Hopefully, these may be just temporary steps in the wrong direction, taken in a hurry, the result of mistakenly deciding that older people are the same as younger adults, and that their needs could be met by ordinary Adult Education courses.

A good educational program for the elderly requires that gerontologists and educationists work together on the design. Consideration has to be given to the fact that elderly people have probably not had anything to do with school for at least forty years: writing papers, taking tests, even copying lecture notes, are essential classroom skills which rust easily. There must also be a sensitivity to the doubts that the elderly frequently repeat to themselves about not knowing enough, or being smart enough — or the worst fear of all — that the minds of older persons deteriorate and so they have lost the ability to deal with schoolwork. But long before the elderly sit down in their classrooms, some philosophical questions should have been raised and answered by the educationists. Why should older people go to school, what should they study and where should it all take place?

Back to School

We send younger people to school to learn how to keep our complex technology and social arrangements in working order. If we are not going to train the elderly for highly technical jobs, should they receive vocational training? Why not? Why can't they be prepared to work in the field of aging where there still are significant numbers of frail elderly people whose needs are not being met? Training for a second career, or even a first one, is good reason for the elderly to attend college and yet it is not being emphasized.

There is enough evidence to indicate that most elderly are not turned on by the invitations to become students at a college of their choice. In response to that snub but convinced that the wish to know is a basic, human impulse, some educationists have designed programs which bring a version of college to the elderly. Thus, in New York, Chicago, Minneapolis, Dade County, Florida, and the state of Iowa, where commitment to this idea is strong, senior centers, nursing homes, churches, and senior residences regularly become classrooms. Those elderly persons who attend the generally one-session-per-week courses tend to be people with very limited education, high school dropouts, not very intellectually sophisticated. Yet classes are attended enthusiastically, the opportunity to be taught by a "professor," which implies profundity, is eagerly seized, and students demonstrate that to live is to learn, while apparently convinced that learning will enhance their living. These courses do not have the rigor of those held on campus, but they are structured along lines which bring into examination matters that seem most relevant to the daily lives and experience of the students. Thus classes will be on current events, with an emphasis on local affairs or the national issues that affect them directly, such as Social Security, mandatory retirement, and health legislation; everyday science also interests, as does an examination of the principles and values of different world religions. This type of program is non-elitist and offers everyone regardless of credentials more to appreciate in life.

However, the type of program which takes the anxieties of the elderly about school and disposes of them by means of sympathetic, realistic counseling, then develops basic reading and writing skills appropriate for college level work, and confronts the students with that level of work, appears to be one of the best models yet developed. A good example is College at Sixty, a division of Fordham University in New York City. The elderly take four seminars in the Liberal Arts for two years in the mainly age-segregated classes; during the second year they take some workshops with younger people. Having been well schooled in both an introduction to the liberal arts and the art and craft of schooling, at the end of two years the students receive a certificate and will automatically be accepted as candidates for regular undergraduate degrees at Fordham. The program is initially properly supportive, yet it always maintains standards, and constantly increases expectations, so that finally the elderly are on their own and can handle themselves among younger students. Neither unrealistic nor condescending, College at Sixty helps its students to grow in assurance, strength and understanding.

This is undoubtedly a confused period in the development of educational programs for the elderly, but the road is not so obscure. Older people are capable of serious, disciplined efforts to attain an educational goal. This strength should guide educationists in their efforts so that a viable new role for the elderly, that of student, may more commonly become the rich source of satisfaction that it is now only infrequently.

Boston, Massachusetts

Charles Niles—Age 83

In 1912 I was working in a woolen mill when Uncle Sam called on me to go to France during World War I. After the War I went back to the woolen mill. I don't want to exaggerate, but I don't remember a day when I didn't enjoy going to work. I never stayed with a job I didn't like. I told my kids, "You get two paychecks in your envelope — one to buy the bacon and eggs, the other to get a little enjoyment out of your job. If you don't get any enjoyment, you might as well drop it." I can't say that I ever stayed with a job that I didn't like, even when I was in the woolen mill.

In those days it wasn't hard to get a better job, and I eventually became a superintendent in a large woolen mill. That doesn't mean as much as it would today because now the job would require background in chemistry or a related field. The "super" or manager is basically a coordinator.

Then the mills slowed production. When the mills get quiet in one place they get quiet everywhere. When one closes down, all the rest do, too. The mill where I had worked was in Connecticut, so I came back home and drifted into selling supplies to restaurants and bakeries. I left that about twenty years ago and went into business for myself, designing and building stores.

When I retired at seventy-six, I had no hobbies. I did have a lot of friends from my business. When you call on them after retirement, they're wonderful to you, but they have their own lives. They're nice to you, but they want to keep on with their own show. So what was I going to do?

I just couldn't sit home and paint as Eisenhower did. By the way, he was my first captain. He was an ensign captain at the time. Mamie used to come to all our reunions, but he couldn't go to every one. Mine was his first command, his real command at Gettysburg. That's why he settled there.

I joined VISTA and went around, rapping on the doors of people over sixty-five and heard their stories. I became involved in going to the legislature, talking to representatives and people in the State House at meetings in the auditorium.

There happened to be an ad in the paper that said anyone over sixty-

Back to School

five could go to Suffolk University, a very nice school right on the hill where I live. The head of VISTA said, "Why don't you go up there. You might learn how to talk properly." I was about eighty when I started going to Suffolk. I took a course on state government, and one thing led to another.

What made me interested in education was what I heard the president of a large company say about what he looked for. At this time his company was bringing in a lot of young college people. He said that he valued his college education for two things: one, that he was able to read a book; the other, that he was able to look at both sides of an issue. I never forgot that.

I'm still going to school. I got a B.S. in communications. If I earn a master's degree, fine. That's one of the advantages I have over the other students — no pressure. When you don't have the strain, things sometimes come out better. I enjoyed philosophy and psychology the best. I think that if I had known about it, I might have drifted into psychology. I might have made about $10,000 a year and been happy. I'm not sure, though, since some of them are begging today.

I cut down on the early hours, because I find that if I don't rush, I'm all set. Now I'm taking eighteen credits, six subjects. Monday I go to classes for an hour and a half, from ten o'clock to 11:30. After lunch, I go from 1:00 until 3:00. On Tuesday I go to class at 7:30 in the evening for three hours. Wednesday is the same as Monday, except that we go to a state prison for debate in the evening. Thursday I have a class at 11:00 and at 4:30 until 7:30. On Saturday I go in for a three-hour class.

I can't say there's anything I like least, even those subjects like biology that I had trouble with. In fact the teacher told me, "You shouldn't feel discouraged, because if you talk a foreign language you only have to know four or five hundred words, not to be a perfectionist, but just to get by. In biology you have to know about a thousand to keep up." That was encouraging. Each course had some nice things about it.

I think in the late 1980s they'll be teaching more older people. There is a difference in education between the old and the young, and since the birthrate is declining and elementary schools are being closed, educational policies will have to change.

I wouldn't be as mentally alert as I am today if I had stayed in the apartment and just looked at TV once in a while. I haven't changed, but I feel a little more content. I like people and although I can't say they like me, I can converse with them and talk intelligently enough to hold my own.

The mere fact that you're mixing with young people is wonderful therapy. That's another of the advantages of going to college. The kids were wonderful. They reminded me of the carpenters and masons I had working for me. When I wanted to do anything, they would say to me, "What do you want done, Mr. Niles?" They knew I would spoil it. The kids couldn't do enough for me. And the teachers were fabulous. I didn't encounter any prejudice in the least. I've been called into classes to talk to my peers.

I had a very interesting experience the other day with a history teacher. He wanted me to come in and talk about the FDR period. I guess he was an FDR buff. I told him a story about Cordell Hull. Many people don't know that when Al Smith ran against Hoover, Hoover beat him easily. When Hoover ran again, anybody that got the Democratic nomination would have become President, no matter who he was. Hull got together with the Southern Democrats and said, "We've got to do something to lick this Smith crowd. We'll get that wishy-washy fellow, the Governor of New York!" The class was surprised. Even the teacher said, "I never knew that!"

I know that some older people are afraid of going back to school. In fact, I used to have a class in English at eleven o'clock. As the ten o'clock class was leaving, I met a lady fifty-five or sixty years old. When she left the first time, she said, "I don't like him." I didn't say anything because I didn't know the professor. About the third time, she was still saying that and I said, "Why don't you like him?" She said, "Oh, he's too critical." I said, "See, you know more than he does. You should be grateful that he's paying attention to you and helping you. If he didn't pay attention, you'd feel as if you were slighted. By correcting you, he's showing his concern." I think they're going together now. Naturally when I went the first year, I'd say the hardest thing to cope with was my hearing. When I get in with three or four people, I can't hear very well. I didn't associate with the kids to find out if one teacher was good in philosophy or another was good in something else, so I just took the courses as they came. I think if I had had that advantage, I might have liked the courses even more, even those I didn't pass.

We do a lot of debating, and I'm on the debating team. Every Wednesday we go down to the prison and debate with the inmates. They pick out the subjects from a list of ten topics. Our last topic was, "Has a person working under someone in the state government the right to speak against him?"

I took part in a couple of debates, but most of what I do is in forensics, speaking about different things. Debating depends on the knowledge of the things you look up, while forensics involves getting up and discussing some topic. If you want to debate properly you have to know facts. You can wave your hands as much as you want, but the judges won't give you credit. I was amazed the first time we went over to MIT. They talked so fast, but they had the facts properly. When I worked, I used something that I had read: "Winning arguments doesn't make sales." I never had many arguments; I just talked about what I had to sell.

I never feel as though I'm so busy that I'm neglecting my family. But somebody asked Margaret about it and she answered, "I tolerate it." She thinks I should act my age. My children complained when I went into VISTA, saying, "Daddy, you've done enough." When you are a volunteer you can choose to quit, but I had no reason to get out.

I do nothing to stay in shape. I walk up to school back and forth, but I'm not like Margaret — she loves to walk. I don't participate in any particular sports. I've been in the hospital with heart trouble so I don't overdo.

I had dreams when I retired of going around the world. Well, I went to Spain. I went to Germany, Norway, and all those places. They've got nothing we haven't got. I like New York, though. I lived most of my life in Belmont, which is a nice place, and people ask me, "How can you move in there with all the crime in the inner city." Well, it happens everywhere.

Strange as it may be, I don't regret death. It's just another epic in life. God has given me good health, and if he's done that, you can get by pretty easily.

New York, New York

Solomon Novick—Age 68

I always felt handicapped because I didn't have an education. In our culture there's a tremendous emphasis placed on education, and you can't divorce cultural expectations from personal feelings. I can't isolate things in myself and say fifty percent was the pressure of the culture and fifty percent was me. I just felt the pressure. The rest of my family went to college, but since I was the oldest child in an immigrant family, I went into the family business to help the others. I married a woman who was well educated, and I have a son who is a teacher on the university level. That was a further inducement for me to get an education. Still, it was purely for my own sake that I've gone to college. I've always felt a need for knowledge and experience.

I retired at sixty-five, three years ago. My retirement wasn't compulsory, but something that I had planned for two or three years before. I had a difficult transition period, though. Even though I knew I was going to retire, the emotional change — getting accustomed to a new lifestyle, no longer earning money — is something you cannot anticipate until you actually retire. My transition lasted six months. I didn't enjoy my business. It was merely a vehicle to make a living and it was hard work. But at first after I retired, I sometimes felt that I had done the wrong thing to go out of business. It was so hard adjusting to everything.

I retired in March and I knew I was going to spend the rest of my life in some aspect or other of education. From retirement until the fall, I spent my time searching for a school. I went to Hunter and NYU, but didn't really like the programs there. I decided to come to Fordham because I had a meeting with Dr. Adamson, who is the director of the College at Sixty. This is a division of Fordham for men and women who are fifty years old and older. The meeting made quite an impression on me. The College offers about twelve different courses, and if you take four courses, one each semester, you get a certificate. There isn't as much concentration and emphasis on papers as in regular college courses, but you do have some papers to write. You have to concentrate and get involved.

College at Sixty is really preparatory; it's like a bridge to college work. The studies pursued there helped me considerably, because at first I found it difficult learning to concentrate, to take notes and do a research paper. I never had the experience that the other students had in high school; I had to go into this stuff cold. It took a lot of adjusting.

When you get your certificate from College at Sixty, you go into the Excel program, which is for afternoon and evening students. It's college work, but not quite as concentrated as in the Liberal Arts College. You take two years of Excel courses, then you pick your major and minor and go automatically into the Liberal Arts College. I'm now at the end of the Excel program and I have to make a decision pretty soon as to my major and minor.

I think I would like to get my B.A. in history or psychology with an emphasis on gerontology. They've just opened an outreach program here, and I would like to become a peer consultant for people my own age. I've had some experience with groups already: encounter groups, TM groups, and so on. I like a group relationship with people, and I'd be able to help people get over the same transition period I went through a little more easily. Some people find it very difficult, and some, unfortunately, never get over it.

The Excel classes are intergenerational. There you'll find people from nineteen to my age. There's a very good rapport among the students. People accept us. I never felt any prejudice on the part of the younger students. They welcome us as part of the scene. I go down to the cafeteria and associate with the other students as though I were a twenty-year-old. It's a wonderful atmosphere.

Adjusting to academic life was very difficult. I'll never forget the first test I took. It was a midterm in psychology and I was very nervous. I didn't do too badly; I got a B in the course. But I demand perfection from myself. I once complained to a professor about getting a B in a course. He said to me, "What's going to happen? Is your mother going to spank you?" I said, "No, I'll spank myself." Even though you're doing the work for yourself, you want to know what kind of progress you're making. You want to be recognized, and that's what the grade means. You have to have an outside way of measuring.

There's a process involved in overcoming the fear of attending college. First, you have to decide that you want it. You have to have an incentive, whether it's the fact that you're being pushed or a notion that you've always wanted to do it. Once you are sure that you want to do it, you have to go about it yourself. I conduct groups in which I sit down with the people and get them to list all their liabilities, assets and interests so that they can successfully choose their goals in college. The academic community will eventually offer anything that you want. Students are consumers. What we consume is education and the university supplies it to us. I show people around Fordham, and bring them into classes. It's a way of getting people interested in College at Sixty. We also have lectures once a week on different topics. It's a way of keeping people occupied and active.

Learning is still difficult for me. We've had group sessions about test-taking, how to prepare for a test, how to write a paper. That's helped me. Occasionally, I do wish I were just going to the movies or playing golf. Human nature just does not run down the same path all the time. Often I have my doubts, and I question why I must wake up at 7:00 in the morning to go to classes. I sometimes ask myself, "Why do I want it?" That's part of the learning process. You have to have doubts. In order for the brain to function, there has to be some tension.

I'm here to learn. The degree doesn't mean that much. The daily process of learning is more important. If I want to take a course that doesn't offer academic credits, I'll take it. If I have to wait another year for my B.A., it doesn't matter. I'm not going on to a career. The process of learning does. There's no doubt that I appreciate learning much more because of my age and experience.

The courses I like the best are those that have to do with current events. I had one course in the history of economics that I enjoyed a lot and was very excited about. I also had a course in culture and community concerning the makeup of communities and the functions of different groups. These kinds of courses relate to contemporary life. When you read the paper, you understand more about what is going on in the world. You don't just read the print anymore; you read what's behind it. "Why?" — You're always asking that question now. "Why did so and so do this? Why did such and such happen?" This is very important to me.

I wrote a paper recently on the Hasidim. It was so exciting to learn about their history, visit their homes and spend the weekend with them. They have a remarkable culture and family life. It was a wonderful experience. I loved it. In a way it gave me roots. I don't know much about the Jewish religion even though I have a brother who's a rabbi. When I was young, I tried to assimilate, and that meant dropping religion. I knew I was Jewish, but I was just nonreligious. Now I'm sorry I did that, especially when I see how interested my son is in the life that his grandparents led in Europe. Even though I was born in Europe and lived there until I was twelve, I can't remember anything about it. At college, I find that I'm able to get in touch with my past again. As someone said, "If you don't know your past, you won't know your future." I'm trying to catch up.

One of the reasons I came to college was to meet people with whom I had common interests. When you're in business you have different interests from the people that you do business with. I was looking for new friends and I found them. I've met a lot of people, and we've become quite close. We go to concerts at Lincoln Center together and try to get involved in things that interest us.

All these new endeavors created a little trouble with my wife. She's accepting now, but it took a little while. She had the idea that once I retired I would spend more time with her, take her to the movies and for walks. That's fine, of course, and I like to do that, but I find my new life more stimulating. She's come around, though. She herself has just retired from teaching and now has a lot of her own interests. She's a musician and attends lots of concerts. She wasn't jealous of me. It was a combination of many, many things. It was a new lifestyle that we had to work out. When I was working she always knew that I left the house at 8:00 and I would be home at around 8:00 or 8:30. There isn't that day-to-day routine anymore. I think we've worked it out pretty well now. She edits all my papers for grammatical mistakes, but she has nothing to do with the writing. She wouldn't do it, and I wouldn't let her because we have different points of view.

I get a lot of support from my son. He encourages me and thinks I'm great. He reads all my papers. Whenever he comes to visit, he always asks to read the latest one I've written. When I give it to him, he reads them and smiles. Outside of a good grade, the thing that gives me the most satisfaction is a pat on the back from my son.

Practically every school has adult education now. Retirees are encouraged to attend. My only complaint, though, is that there aren't enough activities for us. We can't really participate in any of the social activities such as athletics, or even clubs. In a philosophy club that I joined, I wasn't discouraged by anyone, but I felt out of place. In a club, you might have one or two people my age and then nine or ten young people. There should be more clubs and activities for older people, and they should be encouraged to take part in the extracurricular activities. They could have an athletic program, in fact. We could go on field trips. I, for one, would be interested in going to places that I can't visit on my own.

Since attending college I feel that I have more understanding. I was always pessimistic. After all, I was a businessman. But I see now that you can't change history. You can't be moralistic or follow the law to the letter. I always had regrets my whole life, such as not attending college or the kind of life I pursued. Now I don't blame it on anything except circumstance and environment. Just as my son knew he was going to high school and college, I did what was expected of me. There's no such thing as good or bad, better or worse. It's not better that my son went to college and worse that I went into business. We both just did what our parents and the society told us to do.

Chicago, Illinois

Richard Newson—Age 72

I'm back in school again, just for one course. My wife, and I, are going to a night class in glass blowing. She's sixty-eight and I'm seventy-two. I used to have my own electric motor repair business. I retired at my wife's suggestion so that we could travel a little. But that didn't happen. There was an empty store in a building we were buying, and my wife opened up her own business there — an antique shop. In my own store I earned an income, but now she's not paying me a dime. She's operated this shop for about ten years; she loves it, and I go along with it.

I proved in business that I was at least equal to people, but I wanted to improve myself even more. When I was a child in Canada during the First World War, my father was in the Army and there were six children to feed. I left before finishing grade school. I blamed my father because I thought he wasn't interested enough. Then I realized that if I wanted it badly enough, I would get the education.

When I retired I found I had some time on my hands. I didn't know if I would be accepted, but I took the government's test to qualify for college. I passed, and a college wrote me saying that I could take any of 115 different studies as a regular college-level student. It was quite an opportunity, and I grabbed it. I went to Morton College in 1971. After a couple of years, I became so badly crippled with arthritis that I gave it up. Then I got a letter in the mail telling me I had forty-one credits. I figured that with nineteen more, I could get my degree. So I went back to school.

When I was in business, I wrote for mechanical magazines. I had always had a desire to write. I wanted to study journalism at Morton, but a counselor discouraged me because I had done some writing all my life and I seemed to have done pretty well. The advisor, an English professor, told me he didn't think they could advance me too much in the field of journalism. It was suggested I go into general studies. They could teach me other things — geography, geology, psychology. That was quite a challenge.

The first semester was pretty rough. I was sure I wouldn't pass the first test. As for algebra and trigonometry, I couldn't even spell the words. But toward the end a teacher of philosophy asked me to take over the class, and a teacher of anthropology would tell the students to look at my notes when the students came to a difficult question. I'm not bragging, but I had a goal and I far surpassed it. On graduation day, I received the outstanding student award. I didn't know a thing about it. They asked me to come up and accept the award. I was sitting with the kids thinking, "I wonder who the heck that is?" I nearly died. If a person has a bit of sentiment in him he can be moved to tears, and I walked up the aisle in tears. My niece graduated with me — she was seventeen and I was seventy. I enjoyed it. To be honest about it, I'm the kind of person who needs recognition.

I have an A.A. in general studies. They want me to get a B.A. and then come back to school as a teacher or counselor. I wouldn't be an academic advisor, telling kids what courses to take, but I would have an office where I could sit and talk to the kids when they need someone to talk with. I wasn't planning to pursue my B.A., because it sounded like quite a challenge. Let's face it, I'm not a kid anymore, and I'm busy. It just seems like a little too much.

I would like to get back into college because I love the school. It's a new college and the teachers are quite good. Of course, there are always one or two with whom you can't quite attain a good rapport. I would go back into psychology. If I'm still with it, I'll give serious thought to going into counseling. I talk a lot but I can also listen well. When I was at the hospital, one of the nurses came to me with her problems. She told me I really helped. This just might be my niche.

In my business, I had felt acceptance. I never had any training, so I had to teach myself. At times I would be called down to a place like the telephone company for a conference on some knotty little problem that was associated with our work. I was not an engineer, but I had a lot of practical experience. An engineer came down from one of these big places with his motor to be repaired. He had a degree, but the motor had some little bugs in it that he couldn't even see, while they were so apparent to me. It was all so rewarding and satisfying thinking, "Gosh, here are these big men that are making those big salaries coming to me." I enjoyed it.

Older people have a tendency to ostracize themselves. The young people have their own lifestyle and their own manner of living and old people have a tendency to pull away from that lifestyle. I began to feel a need to be with people of all ages. I wanted old people to like me, to want to be around me and come to me every once in a while for some advice or something, but I also wanted the kids to accept me.

I keep up my appearances. When I tell people how old I am, they're suprised because I stay young looking. I credit my youthfulness to being

Back to School

with these young people and accept their way of life as much as I can except for smoking grass. I was invited to a few pot parties, but I didn't go.

In the first semester, I encountered a lot of prejudice on the part of the younger students. They're a pretty nice group, but they're only kids. You can make all these excuses for them, but inside you know they've hurt you terribly. It was really rough for me. I was accused of not belonging — that I must be up to something underhanded. Probably I was a government man making an investigation. Some of the teachers questioned my being there. I had one unforgettable experience. I went to the study hall one morning. The study hall is located in a separate building; I was wearing my new hat, which had cost me $20. Seven or eight of the fellows got together and one of them grabbed the hat. It went all the way around the student center, and they pulled it down around their ears, made funny faces and did all sorts of things. One guy in particular was the instigator. Finally, I got my hat back. I was upset, but I kept it to myself. I wasn't about to make an issue of it, so I laughed halfheartedly and thought, "Well, it's a joke, what am I going to do?" I went through all this and had gotten to the point that I was so discouraged I wondered if I should continue.

The fellow who started it all, the one who hassled me the most the first semester, came in one morning when I was in charge of the college paper. He looked very bad indeed. I said, "Rick, you look mighty bad. I know where you were Friday night because I was invited to that pot party. You still show it." He had taken his first shot in the arm, a mainliner. He looked terrible, secondary reactions. I said, "Rick, why don't you go home. I'm the only one here and more or less in charge. I'll tell them that you became sick right here and I advised you to go home. I insist on it." He looked at me in amazement. While he was standing there thinking it over, another one of the guys came up and said, "You didn't tell this old S.O.B. what went on!" Then Rick said, "Mr. Newson is all right. Lay off him. He's one of us."

The following Christmas, I got a big red card in a big green envelope — the largest Christmas card I had ever received. It was addressed inside "to the nicest old man I ever knew." Who do you think sent it? Rick. It rewarded me for what I went through and brought me back to life. It knocked the discouragement all to hell.

Generally old people are more reserved and quiet in school. They have to be handled gently. Most older people would like a little respect and they hesitate to be outgoing. I think older people are far more sensitive, and make mountains out of molehills, and are open to personal affronts. They have to feel wanted and needed, and they have to be given special treatment. Don't make them feel thay they're alone or they will feel ostracized. You've got to bring them in where they can be part of the show. During a break in classes, in the cafeteria, for example, there are three groups: first, the younger students; second, the seniors; and third, the faculty. They do not generally mix. I used to eat alone most of the time, but before a lunch period was over, I would have five or six kids sitting with me. They would come over and say, "Can I sit with you, Mr. Newson?" That was gratifying.

I was one of the writers and proofers for the school paper. Some of the kids were easily discouraged and I tried to help them out. One of the teachers, the advisor of the paper, did not care for poetry and short stories, but I felt they should be included. Students get so much encouragement from seeing their names in a by-line. The poetry may not be good, or the story may lack something, but that doesn't matter; it's more important to encourage the students. I wanted to have one out of every four issues contain something called the Poet's Corner. Later the advisor was replaced by a woman, who is doing a great job. I want to see the paper become one of the best in the country.

My wife and I have been together for fifty-three years. We talk about death because we're very close to each other and very much in love. We wonder what's going to happen when eventually one of us dies. She tries to flatter me by asking, but what is she going to do without me? In all fairness and honesty, I ask what I am going to do without her. Partly in jest, we wonder if we couldn't go together. That sounds kind of morbid. I read an article about death which pointed out that when one member of a couple dies, the other one follows in a matter of months or even weeks. Why? Because such a big part of your life is gone for good.

My wife and I are not deeply religious, but I have this inner feeling, this inner voice. When I was in traction and in great pain, I would lay my head on the pillow and, not knowing to whom or what I was talking, I would say thanks for a good day. There are times when things are going well for me and I say thanks. Why, I don't know. We're not afraid of death. There's a time and you go, like Crosby singing on the golf course.

Gray Power

An image that will serve to illustrate the political power of the elderly in America, is that of the shy, neighborhood teenager, who having been physically intimidated as a boy, seems unaware, almost afraid, of the enormous size and strength that he has grown to in adolescence. Ignored, discriminated against, ultimately abused, the elderly nevertheless have the potential strength to be a powerful political influence. Not extravagant, when one realizes what a spectacular number of older people participate in the election process. Ninety percent of them vote consistently, which makes the elderly the single largest voting bloc in the country, a situation which they have never exploited to their own advantage. Only in the last few years have the elderly been asserting themselves proudly and taken militant positions on their own behalf. The boys in the smoke-filled back rooms are learning that the elderly mean a lot of votes, which no one can afford to lose.

We insisted for many years that older people should neither be seen nor heard; any message repeated long enough is remembered. It was widely accepted that nothing good could come from being old, and soon gray-haired people were identifying themselves as twenty-one plus. If older people were vigorous, bright, assertive, they were spoken of as youthful, and understandably they, too, preferred that image of themselves. Under strong pressure to be self-denying, the elderly could scarcely reach out to one another in common cause.

The recent breakthrough to political activism took place when a number of people, who had previously been involved in social causes, came of age. Some had organized factory workers in the automobile industry during the early years of the UAW; others had volunteered to fight in Spain against fascism; another group had learned their lessons during the struggle for Civil Rights in the South; the final training ground was the anti-war movement of the Sixties. As more and more of these experienced protesters joined the ranks of the elderly, they increased its organizational strength; consequently there has been less and less quiet submission to Ageism.

Actually, the elderly had attempted to establish political organizations several times during the thirties to promote pension benefits, which the new Social Security Act had not granted them. None of these attempts could gather either sufficient strength or influence to achieve the organizations' goals, and subsequently they faded away. But as the elderly population grew and more issues relating to them emerged, national organizations of the elderly shouted to be born.

There was a response in 1947 when Dr. Ethel Percy Andrus formed the National Retired Teachers Association to work in state legislatures for pension reforms and in Congress for tax benefits. A woman with brilliant organizational talent, Dr. Andrus brought the American Association of Retired Persons into being in 1958, so that all retirees, not merely teachers, could take advantage of the new, innovative health insurance program she had engineered.

Today, AARP is the largest membership organization of the elderly in the country, and possibly only Little League baseball can match its remarkable growth during the past twenty years — from the 200,000 NRTA members it started with — to its current membership of close to 12,000,000. AARP obviously knows what the elderly want and offers it to them in a variety of services.

The health insurance program remains in operation and generates considerable income for AARP, as does a Travel Service that has specially designed trips for the elderly; a pharmacy service makes drugs and medicine available at low prices at retail stores; a Driver Improvement program has helped more than 200,000 older drivers; government grants fund the administration of a public jobs program and a legal aid project; in addition AARP offers consumer advice, sponsors educational programs at colleges and universities, and supports research lobbies for legislation on state and national levels.

AARP has the magnitude and range of a giant corporation. The success of its impressive operation must be due to the meshing of vast, organizational gears — the 2,500 local, state and regional chapters which enable staff headquarters to maintain contact with the membership army. Critics complain, however, that its size and wealth limit AARP's involvement with urgent elderly needs but link it rather to big business interests.

The other mass membership organization of the elderly is the National Council of Senior Citizens; which had its beginnings at the 1961 Conference on Aging. Labor leaders who were there realized that if Medicare legislation were to pass, it would need heavy support from the elderly themselves. Much of NCSC's annual budget is contributed by the labor unions. The early membership of NCSC came largely from their ranks, and

Gray Power

today its above 3,000,000 membership, affiliated with clubs around the country, is still mainly comprised of elderly whose hearts belong to the unions. While NCSC cannot campaign for political candidates because of its tax-exempt status, it is deeply concerned about legislation and it watchdogs Congress, advises its membership about which of the lawmakers votes in accord with NCSC positions, and through its newspaper and special telegrams urges its members to lobby for significant bills. Although its membership is essentially elderly, NCSC claims that it is more than a special interest group and has been involved with issues that affect all Americans. It supported Clean Air bills, the Test Ban Treaty, the Peace Corps, and the War on Poverty. Among the services it provides members are: low-cost travel, discount drugs, and supplemental insurance for Medicare. Occasionally NCSC is caught between its allegiance to the trade unions, which have the interests of younger people to promote, and its elderly membership. The unions may not always be in favor of a position that the elderly take, for example, the latter's opposition to mandatory retirement. Which places NCSC in a dilemma.

If one views AARP and NCSC as suffering from the defects of a centralized power that even the kindliest of giants must exercise, then the Gray Panthers should be regarded as extremely virtuous. For as Maggie Kuhn pointed out in an earlier section, the Gray Panthers have: an informal structure — almost anyone who wants to call oneself a Gray Panther can be one; it has a smallness of size that doesn't interfere with movement; and no government funding, so the Panthers can campaign for any good person around. The organization does not get in the way of its members. With neither dues, business interests, donations, nor a ruling body that establishes policy, the Gray Panthers are free to follow the lead of anyone who has an idea worth following. For the Gray Panthers, process is program, and activism the best political program for an older person to endorse.

Examining the national organizations of the elderly that are involved politically, one sees a rainbow of interests and attitudes, which proves again that all people with gray hair are not alike. It also suggests the need for a new organization.

If a coalition of organizations was formed that would have representation from the full diversity of ethnic, occupational and special interest groups to which the elderly belong, so that all voices and efforts would be united — then gray power could become an irresistible force. Once the elderly can obtain what they need in health care, transportation, housing, and employment and income by the regular exercise of political strength, they will have done much to restore themselves to their entitled place in society. And it is what those of us who are younger should support, because ultimately all society suffers from the despair, guilt, and anxiety that it imposes on any oppressed group. Moreover, since the elderly are so much a part of ourselves — they are our past and our future — resisting their just claims and excluding them from the sources of political power, in effect raises questions about the meaning of our very survival as individuals and as a society. Power to Elderly People!

Philadelphia, Pennsylvania

Jean Hopper—Age 69

I've been an activist all of my life. Before I joined the Panthers in 1974, I was active in helping to develop and organize a union. I've also been active in Philadelphia politics. I was in the anti-Vietnam protest and I've been a member of protest organizations such as the Women's League for Peace and Freedom. I was also active in the Spanish Loyalist cause. I should say my mentor was Will Durant, who brought me into the liberal field. That was my training in a sense.

A few years ago when I was about to retire from my job as a librarian my ex-brother-in-law, who worked with a Nader group that merged eventually with the Gray Panthers, asked me to join the organization. I had been reading a great deal about the Gray Panthers for a few months before, so there was no difficulty in involving me in their cause. I was attracted by their use of the technique of consciousness-raising, with which they attempt to tear ideas out of your mind, turning them upside-down, replacing them with new ideas. I liked that feeling, since I've been trying to do that all my life. I always review periodically the things I stand for, because they may have changed, whether it's the union or anything else. The Panthers harmonized very well with my general attitude.

I'm working at the Gray Panther national office, trying to be the information specialist, gathering all the materials needed to keep the organization up-to-date on developments. I send things to Maggie Kuhn, the founder of the Gray Panthers, because she has to be kept informed. I subscribe to lots of magazines and newspapers and try to read widely to have a broad approach. I do all the basic bibliographies in my free time. I organized their library about three years ago and I'm maintaining it. I answer some of Maggie's letters on specific issues, many having to do with health care, housing and Medicare difficulties. Health care and housing seem to be the basic issues.

Some people have real problems and we try to refer them to the proper person or agency, since we can't solve their problems for them. The library has been very useful. It consists mainly of clippings and pamphlets, but for a no-budget library, it's doing very well. Most of the questions are on Medicare and drugs. People need to be told how to deal with government agencies, either personally or through advocates. The people who write to us, I can tell, are not mobile. They're unsophisticated and unaware of the methods for solving a problem. They need someone — an advocate — who will take them by the hand and take care of them. We're dealing with people who are very much in need of help.

I spend two full days a week at the library in the Panther office, 9:00 to 4:00 or 5:00. If something requires deep thought, I'll take the problem home and work on it. This library is involved with all facets of aging — the aging process itself and aging as it applies to activism, transportation, education, medical care. Since we have task forces in the fields of economic systems, housing, health care and hunger, I also try to develop those areas as general interest.

The library is heavily used, especially by students who are doing research. It has no budget or personnel expenses, but it's a desirable place for students in gerontology to come, because there's no other library which has all this information located in one place. If a researcher went to the University of Pennsylvania, he would probably have to use a number of different libraries. This way, everything is compact and convenient. I did a professional job setting up the place. Since I have a master's degree from Columbia, I should do a creditable job, or I would think that I wasted my money and time.

I am very much interested in the national health service because I think we need it desperately. In analyzing the medical dollar, one finds about fifty to sixty percent going to hospitals. It is important to stress that eight or nine percent of the GNP goes to health care, and we have only acute medical care for the very poor. In Canada only seven percent of the GNP goes to health care which provides lifetime assistance. We shouldn't have to pay more. That's very important. The money is just not being used efficiently. People must be shown that spending more for good health care is unnecessary. The use of hospitals must be cut down, even though many cities have a surplus of beds. Home health care is more important.

I think the bureaucracy in our present health system is a tremendous burden on older people. It's too fixed and too inconvenient. Older people are left out and deprived of the rights to which they're entitled by the complexity and unavailability of the system. That bothers me a great deal.

I feel the same way about the library. If we're going to offer library services we should decentralize them so they are within walking distance of the people. Those feelings and thoughts apply to medical care for older people and about many other services to which they are entitled.

I sometimes feel that things aren't going to get done, but I try hard. I tell Maggie, "I don't want those bastards to think they can get away with it." Some people say to me, "Why don't you let the young people take care of it." I reply, "No, because every day that I live the system has an impact on me." I want to help young people, but I feel injustices very keenly. They deserve a better world than we had. The worst thing is apathy.

One of my young colleagues that I still see had about four candidates for the union that I organized. We talked and I was really able to discuss the issues and whom we needed this time. It was gratifying for both of us. I'm glad I can talk to young people and give them the benefit of my experience, and, I hope, my wisdom.

The main problem about being old is the stereotyping — people stereotype you before they know you. I believe in mixing, people doing things together. Some tend to isolate us, and I resent it. I'm the same individual that I was before I was sixty-five. I haven't changed. I've just had more of a chance to develop myself. I should be better, not worse. Some think that old people are always talking about their aches and pains, that they have no sense of humor, that they're not liberal about sex. We still have the same desires for sex and affection. We haven't changed, maybe just slowed down, but not changed.

What troubles me a great deal is that my peers have accepted these stereotypes. They've been brainwashed by them and are living that type of life. It makes me very, very sad. It's a problem typical of many people.

I've given up on the system as a whole. I'm trying to seek out certain benefits and increments from the system, provided that those benefits are going in the right direction. That's my goal, really. The present system is too difficult and too powerful to try to fight. Let's develop alternative systems. Let's seek out benefits. That's my goal.

You get more detached when you get older and can be a little more objective about things. I am wiser. I don't see every situation as a single thing, unrelated, but in a larger context. If there is a problem, I see all the relationships. This experience has made me develop a philosophy by which I've been able to unify my life.

It's an important thing to keep up with knowledge. I feel that you don't have to be an expert, but you have to be informed so that you can make decisions. I try to keep myself informed on nuclear plants or whatever so that I can make my own decision. I've been very conscious of this recently. You just don't go out and demonstrate; first you do a lot of research and decide if you want to demonstrate and why.

I had a fantastic, unusual childhood. I knew Will and Ariel Durant.

Jean Hopper

My sister was a friend of Ariel, and she used to come to our house. I also spent time in the Community Church. John Holmes was the reader there and a friend of Gandhi's. This church was open to all races, so it didn't have to be integrated. I became very broadminded while I was very young. I also knew Scott Nearing. After World War I, he was fired from the University of Pennsylvania because he was against the war and child labor. He couldn't stay in any political party because he was too much an individual. He had a very primitive place up in Vermont, and my sister and I would go there and stay. He believed in vegetarianism. Recently he was honored by the University of Pennsylvania because he believed in the outdoors and the natural way of living. The young people are following him. The books he published forty years ago are being republished and read. So, in my own lifetime, I've seen fantastic things. I'm able to see my development, ideologically and otherwise, and how I've even reversed myself. To me life is a fantastic panorama that we're facing all the time.

I'm very fortunate in never having encountered any prejudice about my age. Many of my interests cut across age groups. I'm interested in things that young people would be interested in, such as photography and modern dance, and I've been taking courses at Temple University. It's been a multigenerational approach, and I find myself getting along very well. That's because certain interests cannot be categorized as old or young, but only as individual. When I was young I wanted to be able to develop my interests through more leisure time. I wanted to go back to school, which I've done now. I wanted to have the chance to be much more active politically, something which you're often denied when you have to worry about a job or civil service. This limits your ability to do the things you should do as a concerned citizen. By being old I'm actually allowed to become an active citizen without being concerned about all the things that might happen to me. I never resented working, though — I loved it. I was the head of the Business Science and Industry Department of the library. I was one of those fortunate people who never knew where my personal interests ended and my professional life started. They sort of intertwined. I even enjoyed supervising.

Since I've retired my relationship with my family hasn't changed, but I've had more time to see them, and, in fact, my relationship with them has been enhanced.

I'm also active in the U.S.-China Friendship Association. In fact, I'm treasurer this year. I went to China last year for twenty-two days, and in visiting six cities took about 2,000 slides. I've selected about four hundred, as much as people can stand, and I've given slide shows and talks. I'm also

Gray Power

a member of the Association of Retired Professionals. I'm having a fantastic life. Of course, I'm a very greedy person. I have subscriptions to the ballet, the theater and the dance. I really am taking advantage of living in Philadelphia and enjoying its arts. I'm taking a course in music appreciation at Temple, where each week the professor discusses the program of the Philadelphia Orchestra. If I see the program, I'm getting a nice little background to it. I've been taking courses in architecture, not of a technical nature, but of the history of architecture. I'm interested in the ways of applying architecture to the needs of older people. I haven't found the answer. The instructor uses a lot of perceptual psychology in this course. I haven't taken psychology in about forty years, so I'm finding it a little painful, but I'm able to participate a bit.

I'm a photographer. I'm also a physical person. I like to cook. In fact, I call myself a "Renaissance radical" because I enjoy all knowledge. I've followed modern dance my whole life, and the more modern the better. I'm learning to enjoy avant-garde theater. I don't just want to listen to things I know, but to learn new things even if just to dislike them. It's the only way I can grow. I just don't want to wind up listening to eighteenth-century music.

I don't have any regrets. I've gotten myself into situations, but I've never regretted them because I think they actually have helped me grow. Any experiences I've had, even if they've ended negatively, have had a positive effect upon me. I've been able to do what I want, so I'm not frustrated in that sense. Also, I've never made my goals too inaccessible or unrealistic. I've had some frustrations when I've worked on projects like "Recall Rizzo," that we lost. Politically I've been unhappy, but that's a general thing, not a personal one.

I underwent a mastectomy this year, but I'm not worried about dying because I'm too involved with what I'm doing. I really don't think about it. Of course, I've made some plans. I have a will, and I've joined a memorial society. I've done everything to see that my survivors won't have too many problems. I even cleaned out my home so that they won't have to go through thirty years of accumulation, just six months' worth.

I'm dealing with the effect of death right now. I've been undergoing chemotherapy twice a month. The treatment makes me nauseous for a day, but I overcome it. My doctor wants to see how effective the therapy has been, so I've been through a lot of tests. I'm not sure how much longer I'm going to live, but I'm still doing things. I'm going to Cuba. My physical condition bothers me, but not to the extent that it pervades my whole life. I feel fine now, but this type of thing is so insidious. I try not to find pat answers. I'm not waiting. I just want to keep on doing things.

San Francisco, California

Francis Brown—Age 75

I've been working with the elderly for about eight years as a volunteer, I'll be seventy-five in October. I have to do something; I can't just sit home and read. I've always been active in politics as a progressive, and I'm very good at organizational work. During World War II I was a member of the American Legion Against Fascism. I've worked with the trade union movement and still do.

I became interested in this work because someone I knew well in Massachusetts spoke out here before a group which was trying to organize the elderly. I was elected Membership Director for two years, organizing the California Legislative Council for Older Americans. I think we have about two hundred thousand members in California, including union people. We're also affiliated with the National Council of Senior Citizens, which has about three and a half million members. I don't agree with everything they do. It wouldn't be my way. I don't like to go begging from the government. The elderly helped build this country, and I feel they are entitled to certain things. It's really their right to have a decent life. The elderly are at the end of the line and shouldn't have to worry about money. They should not be on a fixed income. They should have decent housing, national health security, preventative medicine, not just finding cures.

Working with the elderly is different from the organizing I did before, because trade union members are knowledgable, informed people. When I started working with the elderly I found they lacked information. Also some of them would get tired of struggling and even tired of living. There were many suicides. We formed a suicide prevention organization, which has helped.

If there hadn't been a progressive movement, there wouldn't be an elderly movement. You have to be a progressive person or a very strong liberal to undertake a job like this. You cannot separate politics from everyday living. This is a fact. If I hadn't always been an activist, this would be the last thing I would do, because from the beginning it was a formidable job; it still is. It's difficult to organize housewives who never worked, had no experience with a trade union and who maybe even used to protest when their husbands would go to union meetings. They worked in their homes, for their families, but not in the outside world.

Gray Power

I don't think there is as much prejudice against old people now as there was. It's in a much milder form. For example here in California we have worked for twenty years to repeal a bill that was passed twenty years ago requiring children to support their parents and grandparents. I think that bill created prejudice. You can't force families with small incomes. They have children to support, they can't take on parents and grandparents. Especially now. Since I have been working with the elderly, we have every year taken up the question of repealing the bill. Last year we were successful, and they repealed it. That should make a difference.

Knowledgable young people are doing a marvelous job as far as the elderly are concerned in California. We have spoken at universities, and the students take an interest in what we are doing. The community colleges have several senior groups. There's a lot of work connected with educating people so they can do their own work.

Right now the important issues are national health security and housing. Our priority this year is health security. We're trying to have the Kennedy-Corman bill passed. The passage of the bill looks very slim. By the time it gets out of committee we won't be able to recognize it. It isn't a great bill. It has a lot of shortcomings; it doesn't cover dentures, or glasses, or nursing care for the aged. But we're hoping they'll pass it.

We don't advocate nursing homes; caring for people in their own homes is preferable. I find it's traumatic for the elderly to be moved out of their own homes into a nursing home. They don't live very long.

I hope to see the Tenderloin District rehabilitated so that the seniors can live in better housing. I'm objecting very strongly to moving them out because in Haight they moved the seniors out while they rehabilitated the housing. Then they were not able to move back in because the rents were so high. We want rent control and subsidized rents in the housing we're planning now so that won't happen again. We're having trouble with Hastings House. They want to build a big office on the land they bought. But I think we've been victorious. They decided to build only part of the building. We also strongly object because they're throwing a lot of people out. A group of us met with the board, and we made proposals to have a multicenter built which seniors would be able to use. There should be a library with newspapers from all over the world. San Francisco is a melting pot. And there should be a kitchen for seniors to cook and entertain. They agreed to it. So we are doing pretty good work.

What I enjoy most in my work is a good fight, whether it's in Washington, D.C., or Sacramento. Last year on May 17 we had about 5,000 people go up on the Hill and really talk to them about national health security. But it's like everything else, you go home and nothing happens. But people are beginning to learn that no matter how much the politicians talk, how many promises they make, when they get elected, they just renege. However, they always want your support. They held an election in San Francisco. In my district there were eleven people running for supervisor, and all eleven of them wanted my endorsement. They want the senior vote. President Carter was here and he said he'd help, definitely, but he reneged. Why? Does it cost too much money? It doesn't. Comprehensive health or preventative health will cost less money in the long run. We have to make our legislators understand that. Whenever anybody gets really sick, it's a very expensive proposition. Of course my feeling is they can conserve money in other ways, not from the health of the elderly or the poor. They can cut the defense budget and instead of building a neutron bomb, spend the money on health care. So much is being published concerning the power of the other nations—building a fear that any minute they will come over and drop a nuclear bomb on us. Spend the money to create more jobs and that will cut crime too.

In this society, where there is so much money and you see people going around hungry, it kind of opens your eyes and you figure you have to do something about it. I try my best to change things, to make them work. If they are not successful, I'm not successful. I have to try something else. I can't quit. That's never been my way. You don't look back; you cannot afford to look back; you have to go forward. There's got to be a way out and you have to look for it.

My mother and father are the people I admired most. I believe the same way that they did. They were progressive people in the union struggle. There were eight people in the family. We believed in a better life for those who produced and those who built. You wouldn't have a world, you wouldn't have anything if these people weren't living and building and doing things. These are the people who don't get anything out of the world. They're exploited. They're underpaid, underfed and underhoused; their health is very poor. If they had some sort of a health program here, a national health program, better housing, a lower cost of living, this would be a great country to live in. A real heaven. That's what we could have.

I don't have any financial worries. Maybe that's why money doesn't faze me. I don't center my life on money. I never did. You need money to eat, to pay the rent, to go on vacations. But that's it.

Gray Power

I relax a great deal. I have always read quite a bit. I go to the theater. I go to concerts occasionally when I have the time. I'm not a moviegoer. I like the legitimate theater.

I didn't worry about growing old when I was younger. I had no time. I still don't have the time. Reverend Williams had a birthday the other day. I have known him for a long time. I said to him, "What are you, fifty-five, or forty-four?" He said, "Forty-eight." "My gosh," I said, "getting old." The time has gone so fast. He says he has been here eight years. I told him, "Keep going the way you are and you'll never grow old." He said, "I'll do exactly what you do." I said, "That's not a bad idea."

I'm not afraid of death. When it comes, it will come. Why should I fear it? We don't have much knowledge of it. I'm not religious. I think people who fear death haven't done much with their lives. I have tried my very best. I have been successful in a lot of things. But I feel when the end comes it will be all right with me. I can face it. I hope not to be very ill, not to become a burden to anybody. That I wouldn't like, but death doesn't mean much. It will come to everybody, I'm no exception.

I haven't changed towards people; and people haven't changed. But they're beginning to learn that some changes have to be made. This is the richest country in the world, yet we have so much hunger and unemployment. It feels pretty good to see the elderly—the unorganized, willing to go on the picket line and willing to go fight for their rights. Of course, I hoped all my life that I would see changes in this country, but it doesn't seem that way. Not in my time. But I'm hoping that my children, my grandchildren, my great-grandchildren will see it. It's got to come.

Detroit, Michigan

Jack White—Age 69

I've been retired three years. I'm a former trade union activist from the organizing days of the UAW, Walter Reuther's local. I served in the Navy during World War II. I went to the UAW convention in 1946. I opposed the election of Reuther. Having lost that round, I worked on a left-wing newspaper until that folded. Then I went to work in a mine and ultimately ended up with the Teamsters. I've been a truck driver, business agent, publisher, editor of a paper, handyman, all kinds of things.

Currently I'm trying to build a national retiree movement in the Teamsters Union. I'm a member of the Mayor's Senior Citizens' Commission. I'm a board member of the Area Agency on Aging. I'm a state board member of the National Senior Citizens' Council and vice-chairman of the Metro Council, and chairman of the Senior Leadership Group which aspires to be a think group.

I had little formal education. I never read a great deal. As a child I was always exposed to ideas, though I was raised in a devout Irish Catholic family. I used to work for a milkman, and I think this man had a lot to do with shaping my life. He was always in a hassle with an authority figure in the church, one or another. Though he was crippled, he did an enormous amount of reading. I would make a remark about some Catholic dogma and he would probe and make me think it out. With other questions, too. He stimulated my interest in philosophy and history. But it was my involvement in activism that educated me, enlightened me, made me what I am. It's been great. I wouldn't trade it for anything.

I first got into activism when I went to work in 1927. My father was a trade unionist and had strong feelings about it. The federal government recognized the right to organize in the thirties.

In 1929 when I was eighteen I was working in the General Motors plant and was distressed about the manner in which we were paid. I listened to a few radicals. I came to the conclusion that we ought to do something about it. About seventeen of us marched into the superintendent's office. So I was fired. My father was upset; he claimed I would be blacklisted and never get a job again. Later I went back to work for that same place.

Gray Power

I became frustrated and embittered. In 1934 I took a weekend off to get married. We worked seven nights a week, about thirteen hours a night. I asked for the night off and was told to be there. I took it off and I got fired. I threatened to take it into my own hands by dealing with the person responsible for the discharge, and when he heard about it, he took me back.

In general, labor's attitude toward older people is coming around. The Teamsters were among the last. There is now a retiree's department within the Teamster's organization. But some aspirants for power are viewing it as something to exploit. We are trying to build an advisory council as the UAW does. In the Teamsters you are an honorary member. You're put on the scrap heap. In the UAW you have a vote in the convention and continue membership and participate in the making of some policy. But they are one of the only unions that allows that. The Mineworkers have that, but it works negatively. The corrupt leadership that preceded the present leadership used the retired people as pawns in the local union to maintain themselves in office.

There's a great deal of difference between my activist days and my retired days in fighting for people's rights. I was in on the ground floor. There's been a lot of activity since 1965, when the Older Americans Act was passed. So I came into something full-blown rather than planting the seeds as I had to when I was young. Some of us who are working to improve things are in our sixties, but we still have a lot of energy. We are what makes it go.

I address myself to the constitutency which is economically deprived. They are very hard to reach and move and organize and involve, because people get worn out and totally despondent, they don't believe anything and are listless. We have people living on less than $200 a month from Social Security.

Two things have more of an impact on senior citizens than anything else: the cost of medical care and the cost of living. The utility thing the last couple of winters has exacerbated things. Congress had appropriated money for housing for the elderly, but there was no disbursement money. Most of those people had probably mortgaged themselves to pay their utility bills anyway.

Today I went out to see my mother, who is in a nursing home. She's ninety-two. We're paying out of her reserve of money, $8,000, at the rate of about $800 a month. She is already terrified by the idea that she is going to be on Medicaid in a few months. She said she believes she is already being treated as if she is on Medicaid. She's heard so many horror stories about it.

I think the women in my family have pushed me into looking at things realistically. I always assumed women had a place in society, but it was always serving at the table. My first wife used to tell me there's an enormous gap between my theory and my practice. I had become a member of a small cadre of men in the auto plant; we were a minority among a preponderance of women; and I had all daughters and no sons, and out of seven grandchildren, all were granddaughters until the last one. I've noticed that about 60 percent of all bodies in the auto plant are women, but they are not in the leadership. We're raising hell about this. At age sixty-five a woman is going to live seven years longer than I am. There are 143 women for every 100 men. They say that will dimish somewhat.

I think the worst thing has been the attitude toward older people. I can imagine how blacks must feel, and how women must feel. "You're a nice old man, you really ought to take it easy." It's like you're on the junkheap. And time is against us. Everyday I wake up and find one of our cadre in the obituary page. Unlike other constituencies, we don't have time on our side. But I'm not a person easily put down. I have great trouble thinking of myself as old.

Now I think there's growing recognition of older people, although presently we don't have much input. We're a new constituency and we must become a potent force in the political process.

The most gratifying experience in working with the elderly has been helping to change the attitudes I've been complaining about. I always wanted my children to be liberated, and a lot of women need liberating, too; it's not just the men. But nothing ever changes without a struggle, and I don't expect it will be appreciably changed in my lifetime.

Morgantown, West Virginia

Alice Van Landingham—Age 73

I haven't ever really retired. I just retired from a paying job. My work has just changed in nature. I think women don't necessarily retire. We're homemakers and have many avocations. Until my children grew up, I always had to combine two careers, home and outside work.

I've had such a wide range of interests since college, when I was interested in boy-girl relationships and sex education, which at that time was a bad word. Now they're talking about all the homosexuals — but there have always been a lot. And now more and more women and men in nursing homes are being allowed to get together. There's the story of the nursing home attendant who went to a supervisor and said, "I just saw Bill Jones in bed with Molly Smith. What do I do?" And the supervisor said, "Go back quick and shut the door." We must not segregate the sexes, no matter how old.

In my early years when my children were young, I worked on child development. I supervised physical education in school. I did work on health councils. I've taught in Agricultural Extension's Four Generations groups. Most of the older people I knew were not especially depressed. I've always been interested in people. I've always liked to work with people no matter what their problems. I'm just continuing what I've always done.

I became interested in retired people, so I shifted and did volunteer work with the elderly. Then I became involved with the American Association of Retired Persons. Anyone fifty-five years of age, regardless of sex and income, can become a member of the AARP. We're reaching out and including many people. Social workers are striving hard to get money to serve the elderly poor, but about seventy-five percent of all people over sixty-five can well take care of themselves. Only about four or five percent are in institutions. Twenty percent may be on the poverty line. When I was a volunteer at the senior center, at first many people would say, "Oh, I don't want to join those old people down there." But that's changed.

I became a state director for the AARP. Then I went into committee work. I worked on retirement plans. I had served on advisory committees, in leadership training. Eventually I became a second vice-president.

Alice Van Landingham

The greatest problem is training people. At first people were reluctant to get involved in AARP. My selling point to bring people in is that they see they need something to do. You can only fish so long. You can only travel so long. We have state training and local training. The best way to involve people is to invite them to serve. The secret is to have a scouting group that knows the talent of individuals. The head of the local chapter was a grocer who could hardly walk. And to see him take over and enjoy the leadership was a satisfaction. It's wonderful to see how well people who have been in Rotary and the Lions work in. My greatest satisfaction at AARP is the press. They come and are so interested in seeing these people enjoying themselves.

The most exciting thing I've done is to go to the United Nations Association meeting. I was honored as a national president by the United Nations. About one hundred and fifty of us national presidents of organizations were honored.

Another wonderful thing was to go to Madrid to meet with the Board of Directors of the International Federation on Aging. A fallacy common in many countries is to think that building big buildings to house the elderly is the answer. But the problem really is to have a way of continued involvement.

The AARP involves about ten million people. Our AARP office is in Washington, D.C. We have a paid staff of six hundred-seventy people. When I was president I went to Washington every two weeks or once a month. I'm about an hour away, in Morgantown, West Virginia. I went to Washington for meetings — Advisory Committee, Board of Directors meetings. I spent about half of my waking days on my job, either writing or planning on behalf of AARP. There are six area conferences, and I went to them all. I am now president ex-officio. For two years I will be called on by people who need me.

The greatest part of living is to stay involved and put one involvement on top of the other. As long as there's a need for me, I'll stay involved. But I have things of my own I can always do, straighten out my own affairs. I enjoy family and homemaking and neighbors and local work.

I don't feel I'm patronized as an older person; when you act as an individual you're treated that way. I love to share with reporters the common problems that affect society.

My greatest satisfaction in life was helping to found a nursing home. I helped change one from a dirty, buggy place, through a board of directors and an auxiliary of local women in the community. It was both private and public. There were some problems with the administration. But if you have a cause, the problems can be solved. We incorporated with a Board of Directors and took it over in 1947. I went out there about another matter recently and found it still going strong, thirty years later.

And the senior center is another satisfaction. I've influenced people by improving and introducing activities. I helped start bowling. This is the way to get people just recently retired into other activities. They go from bowling into ceramics, weaving, carpentry.

I'm always involved in community work. Recently I got involved with the new city charter; I made a statement on its behalf.

I had a great experience working with West Virginia's Older Women's Groups. I was invited to come and become a discussion leader. Over four hundred women showed up. We discussed their future problems. Younger women were there, too.

I travel a lot for AARP. My husband went with me when he wanted to. He's great. He was retired in 1972. When he has to travel, I go with him if I can. He was taken into the West Virginia Agriculture Hall of Fame.

Whatever problems my husband and I have had are diminishing. He didn't like AARP much at first, but now he thinks it's a great organization. Still he's happy that my turn is over. When he traveled he said to me, "We're having times we couldn't buy." He helps me; I call him my consultant. He does a lot of reading for me. When he was a professor and attended meetings, I used to go with him as his spouse, and now he comes to meetings as my spouse.

We have three of the greatest children. When my sixteen-year-old got to be twenty, he said, "You'd be surprised how much my old man's learned the last four years."

We help younger people, too. Generations' Alliance is a group of older people meeting with a group of young community people and discussing societal problems, abortion, marriage, whatever. The younger people have vision and we have vision plus wisdom. It's the younger people who want our involvement. We only started the program for discussion purposes and changing attitudes, but the younger people want to extend it.

The intergenerational work started about six years ago in Chicago. The girls in a college out there and some of their boyfriends went out to the nursing homes. They started wondering about all the other old people. I went to Chicago to see if the intergenerational approach would work for us. We took these programs as a model for AARP. We brought in a student, Betty Jane Manconi, who had set up fifty of these chapters on her own. That's how our AARP program, Generations' Alliance began.

Anytime I have an opportunity to go to the medical college and talk to the students, I grab it. I talk to them on the great need to change the whole lifestyle of our society. I think revenue-sharing should be extended to develop leadership, not just for constructing streets and buildings. Mandatory retirement will go by the board. I don't think money is important because if you get sick enough, there's no difference between you and a welfare person. Our educational curriculum should be changed to include teaching use of leisure, attitudes, and spiritual well-being, regardless of religion.

As a young person, I thought if you worked hard and were honest, you'd do all right. You've got to be more than that. You've got to be convinced and dedicated. You're the only one who can help yourself. Now I think there are ways of going in the back door, to help bring out the best in people.

I think we have many more retired people working in the communities now. In our AARP chapter we have people who can teach dancing and art. There is the foster grandparents program. We have the young helping the poor elderly, and we have the elderly working with the young. This is the way back.

AARP has social occasions, but our programs are the greatest. We have a widow's program that includes recently widowed people who then help other freshly widowed people to become involved in the community. We're getting involved in community work. We're founding senior centers. By the way, I don't want to refer to senior citizens; I'll refer to them as older Americans.

I don't have too much time for work with the young, but if invited I'll go to a community 4H group and make a speech.

People with sixty-five years' experience ought to make a contribution. The greatest satisfaction is to see people do things beyond their own capacity, to see people come together. There are more couples now than ever, and the men are really coming in. They want to expand their own lives.

In older people I sense fear of crime, but not fear of dying. Not being afraid myself, people respond to me that way, because I'm fearless and I tell them so in my speeches. That's the last thing we should be afraid of.

I'm not afraid of dying. I have great faith and belief in continuation of life after death. I have some dear friends who don't, but I believe it. If I had an illness, I could stand pain, but I would hate to feel I'm a burden. And I want to stay in my own quarters, even if there's suffering and sacrifice. I would never want to move away from this community and the people who have know me in different stages. When you're in my community I hope you feel free to come and have a cup of tea with me. This is what's important to me.

I believe in the joy of living.

Portland, Oregon

Ruth Haefner—Age 83

I've had lots of interesting experiences. I grew up in Iowa and went to the University of Iowa, graduating in 1918. One of the first jobs I had after graduation was working with women in the local county on wheat conservation for the war effort. This was my first experience in learning to organize women. A few years later I got a job in Chicago with the United Charities and had an opportunity to visit Hull House and meet Jane Addams. At that time the University of Iowa was working on a very unusual project called the Iowa Child Welfare Research Station. Some of the money for the study came from the Rockefeller Foundation. Because I had experience with rural people, it was decided that I should be the first to direct something called "field work." After two years, the Rockefeller people were so impressed with our organization that they set up similar centers all around the country. We tried to study children in all phases of life. One of the men from the Rockefeller Foundation asked me to go with him through the entire country, observing, but I was very young and I had been doing many jobs beyond my capacity. I grew very tired. Meanwhile, my father had moved West, so in 1927 I decided to take a year off, visit my family and rest. I never returned to Iowa.

I was living with my brother, a forester, when he was transferred to Portland. Those were very interesting times in Portland, with politics in a state of flux and the Longshoremen on strike. The Organization of Woodworkers was becoming prominent, and I became involved as a lobbyist for it in the state legislature. I was a supervisor of the census in 1940, and an alternate delegate to the Democratic National Convention in New York.

I became interested in doing volunteer work. I became involved in the NAACP and I've worked with them continuously since 1938. We put through one of the best civil rights laws in the country. I've had a great deal of experience in the legislatures and with minorities. I began to realize that once I was working for one minority, I could use the same techniques to work with other minorities.

Ever since I began doing volunteer work, I've felt there were more things printed than people would be able to read. For about twenty years I've had articles reprinted, particularly those by Norman Cousins. I send these articles everywhere and I've used the same technique with the Panthers, sometimes being called a propagandist.

I'm ashamed to admit that up until three years ago, I had very little interest in senior programs. I didn't think I was getting old, and the programs I saw around town didn't interest me. It seemed their activities consisted of going down to some center and sitting around the piano. That was the situation for about twenty years. I had some interest in the elderly poor, but I didn't become involved. I thought they were pretty well taken care of because of all the publicity they got.

About two years ago, I was asked to serve on the League of Women Voters' human resources committee. We were making a study of the elderly poor, so we visited agencies around the city to learn about their activities. The greatest influence on changing my attitudes toward the elderly was a speech by Maggie Kuhn. She came here in December of that year, and appeared on a local television show. The producers of the show wanted to have a panel consisting of a cross section of people, both old and young. I was asked to be on that panel, and so I met Maggie. I thought I was going along through life having a good time until I heard about the Gray Panthers. It's changed my whole life.

When I read items in the paper that I thought would interest Maggie, I would send her copies of the articles. She made me the "convener" of the Gray Panthers in Oregon. A few of us got together and started an entirely new organization, because we realized that we would get nowhere taking over an old organization or organizing in a senior citizens center. We thought those people were more or less satisfied with what they had. We had to start from the bottom, by throwing out the old conventions like by-laws and *Robert's Rules of Order*. We decided to operate by consensus.

A radio announcement was made of our Saturday morning meeting. The turnout was really surprising, and soon we had a fairly large ongoing group. Some of the people were there for selfish reasons such as parents in nursing homes, or their own personally upsetting experiences in nursing homes. Others had just retired, and many had never done any political work at all. We had one emergency meeting after another. We never wet-nursed anybody. Some people liked our methods, and those that didn't just stayed away. We were so busy with our own organizing that we never learned about the tenets of the National Board of the Panthers because we never had time to contact them. It worked out all right, though. I think our success lies in the lack of formal organization.

Our first project after we were organized was to make a study of nursing homes. I had never been interested in nursing homes, and I didn't like visiting them. Soon after we started this investigation, we had a couple of scandals here, and a few real tragedies occurred. Some people in the homes were "murdered" — you have to use that word because of the poor service they were receiving. The work was very gratifying for us, because we struggled to get the news media to accept that story. I must give them credit. They reported that story like they would any other crime.The story appeared on the front page, in fact, and it said, "The Gray Panthers were there." We conducted a very intensive campaign, and it's still going on.

Now that we have the nursing home task force so well organized, I don't really have to participate in the project anymore. We got the nursing home legislation passed. We've gotten some good people elected to the legislature, but our problem now is to get legislation enacted. People have tried time and time again to get good laws on the books, but the proposals are turned over to something called a human relations committee. We've had citizen participation in all these committees, but it became just ridiculous. The organizers persuade an old person to be the figurehead, and then they do nothing. As soon as a group becomes a governor's committee, you may as well forget about it, because nothing happens unless the governor wants something to be done. I'd like to start a task force for reforming bureaucrats.

The biggest satisfaction in my work comes from being able to do something. When I talk to older people, I tell them, "Don't do anything that you don't like. You've had to do that all your life. Now is the time to enjoy what you're doing." I've seen so many people coming to life and really getting interested in things for the first time. People who have never written a political letter to anyone in their lives are having their letters printed in the paper.

These were people who had recently retired and were looking for some other activity. There was one older woman who singlehandedly researched the nursing home problem in California and got a law passed through that state's legislature. The same experience happened to me. I knew nothing about nursing homes. Now I've participated in training sessions for activities directors of nursing homes.

I always have young people around me. I don't think I would be involved in this work if I were working with only older people. The young people that I meet are wonderful, and I have great faith in them. We will have a new society when they take over. I have talked to many high school and college classes, as well as to young people in institutions for juvenile offenders. My first encounter with a group of young people took place in a

Gray Power

communications class at the University of Portland. They set up a miniature "Meet the Press," and four or five youngsters interviewed me. It was a lot of fun.

When you look back at your life, there are certain big episodes — starting school, learning to read, graduating from high school or college. A very interesting thing has happened to me since I've turned eighty. I think I've had just as much intellectual and social experience in the last two years as I've had in any time in my life.

First, I've been on TV a lot and have gotten very comfortable and good at it. I've been told that I get by very well. Somebody asked me how I could do so well without ever having had any training. I never even belonged to the Toastmasters Club! I've also been asked to speak many times, and I was never trained for that, either. I used to be scared to death, and I worried about the speeches, but I would start talking despite my nervousness. Now I've been told I'm a very dynamic speaker, so I don't worry anymore. I've also been very well accepted by the women's movement, including those more liberal than I. I give workshops at the women's conferences held here occasionally. This year, I told them I didn't want to lead workshops; I wanted to attend them instead.

I was the youngest in my family, and I never really had to face death. Thinking about death was something I always avoided. My parents passed away after short illnesses, and I always hoped to die the same way. I found that death was easier to handle than I had thought. Then about two years ago, my nephew George died, and I was really shaken. I've thought a lot about his death. He was sixty-two — far too young to die — and at the height of his career. One of my other nephews told me that I was so upset because I had always expected George to outlive me. We're working on a memorial for him now. He was a doctor, and I thought I would start a fund to supplement the cost of a medical school education for a poor boy. We're still working on the final arrangements. When he died, I had to face all the things that have to be done—something I had never done before. That seems incredible for someone my age.

I have so many things to look forward to. I want to watch my grand-nephew grow up. I want to work with the Panthers to help solve the problems of a guaranteed national wage and health program. I've had so much joy and so many privileges in my life, far beyond anything I've deserved. Sometimes I feel like I'm Cinderella; I just think that the clock will strike twelve and I'll disappear.

Life at the Center

Leaping and bounding in the proverbial style of growth, the multipurpose senior center, which entered the stage of American institutional life a little more than thirty years ago, is now a fixture. It plays a role in the affairs of the elderly that is gaining importance as the number of senior centers steadily multiplies. There is a great demand for them by the elderly, who know a good thing, as well as what they like.

A place to meet other older people and make friends, a forum for opinion and discussion, a channel for efforts toward improvement in the lot of the elderly, a provider of health services and vital information — this catalogue partially describes some purposes of the multipurpose senior center. An older person entering its doors will also find recreation, education, transportation, employment, entertainment and communal dining. On an average day, a good center is a buzzing, kaleidoscopic hive.

Centers come in various sizes, shapes and places — some unusual and not all good. In cities they are located in housing projects, churches, synagogues, Y's, community centers and settlement houses. Other locations around the country include old school buildings, abandoned firehouses, factories, and unused college dormitories. Often the facilities are limited by lack of funds and cannot service the needs of their members. One center, however, is a jewel and its glitter provides hope for all who dream of what could and should be.

From the top of its modern, three-story, $3.8 million, brick and glass building, designed specifically to accommodate the elderly down to its spacious auditorium and swimming pool, the Waxter Center in Baltimore is the very model of a senior center. No old firehouse, this place. Open seven days a week — probably the only center in the country with enough money to do that — Waxter offers a big bundle of recreational, social and educational programs — which occasionally includes a wedding. Additionally, members can receive dental and podiatry treatments, as well as

Life at the Center

the screening and therapy for visual, hearing and speech problems. The Waxter Center building, budget and programs should be replicated at least 5,000 times.

While the services available to the elderly at a center are apparent, they are the iceberg tip of deeper, emotional needs that are also being addressed. They signify community, the interplay of feelings when space is shared, the outer, physical space — and more importantly — the inner space of concerns, interests, and values. It is a sense of belonging and being cared about, a trust that, if necessary, here one will be cared for.

Today a sense of community is not too common among most Americans of any age. Yet the elderly have been more deprived of its satisfactions than have younger people, not only for the typical Ageist reasons, but also because community was a "given" in the America of their youth.

Now the picture often looks like this: the children are grown and departed from the house; the neighborhood is utterly changed — familiar buildings, stores, homes no longer exist; friends have either moved away or have died, and a younger generation, mostly new to the neighborhood, is disinterested in their opinions and wishes. Alienation comes fast under such conditions, and the elderly begin to doubt that they still belong there.

While not all of the approximately five million older persons who attend senior centers would identify with that bleak picture, many do. For them, the center adds a lot of bright colors to living. Once inside a center, the elderly become valued people who will be neither ignored nor neglected. The loss of old friends may be compensated for by making new ones from among the hundreds of elderly people to be met at lunch, a card game, dance, discussion, or class. Many, describing the importance of a center in their lives, speak first of how it ended loneliness.

There are other supports. The Chinese puzzle of bureaucratic problems affecting the elderly can be reduced by a center's concerned staff. It is comforting to know that when the small print looms too large, there is a friendly expert to help. Further, invited into the decision-making process at the center, the elderly contribute to the shaping of program and policy. Knowing that what they think and say is regarded seriously, center members feel relevant.

The new-found strength nurtured within the center's community frequently leads to involvement with the larger community outside. It seems less the threatening, strange outside, and more the place one has lived for a long time. Soon the elderly are ready to join with other age groups in the community and search for solutions to problems facing all, such as crime in the streets. Thus, for those elderly who initially came to and from the center along icy roads of alienation, the thaw begins.

Loneliness and alienation, those twin perils of the spirit today, were reasons for opening the William Hodson Community Center as the nation's first senior citizen center. The time was 1943, the place New York City and

Life at the Center

the sponsor was the city's welfare department. Before the 1950s began, two more senior centers were in operation, both located in California. While the Hodson Center received its funding from a city governmental agency, the two California centers were financed by private, nonprofit organizations. Today the money story is similar: most senior centers are funded by the government, others by the private sector, while a considerable number balance their budgets by obtaining funds from both.

Of course, there were no handbooks around in the 1940s offering useful hints on how to build a bigger and better senior center, so the early pioneer workers suffered the usual frontier pains of learning from trial and error. The lessons learned back then are still worth learning. Very simply, the activities and services that a center offers evolve from the needs of its members, who should have the loudest voice in deciding which needs will be served, and how.

Individual multipurpose senior centers vary considerably in style and content. What happens in a center depends on who the members are — cultural background, ethnicity, socio-economic status, level of education — the intricate mix of the obvious and the intangible that influences what any human being chooses to do. The members in one center may prefer Bingo, rummy and movies; those in another, Yoga, poetry and French classes, while a third center may choose from both Group A, and Group B, or even create an entirely new menu. This flexibility, this commitment to the will of the membership, is a large reason why the multipurpose senior center is attractive to the elderly and has an assured future.

Subsequent generations of the elderly will be better educated and more affluent than any thus far, which makes it difficult to chart a horoscope for the centers of the future. They will be different, certainly, but whatever they're like, they will continue to exist. For the senior center is where the elderly are to be found. And since the government has recently acknowledged that the center is a focal point, the best way of delivering needed services and communicating with the nation's elderly, the market is definately bullish.

The legislators did not come by their understanding of senior centers mystically. It resulted mainly from the steady flow of information, frequently unsolicited, that the National Institute of Senior Centers had tirelessly been providing. Were awards to be given for senior center image-shaping, then NISC, founded in 1970 as an organization of professionals within the National Council on Aging, would be the winning stylist. Research, "how to" publications, training sessions, a national communications network with senior centers, and an ongoing dialogue with the policy makers in Washington are the means by which NISC gets the job done — helping more centers come into being and achieve excellence.

Occasionally, debates still take place on the value of senior centers. The comments on the following pages voiced by several enthusiastic el-

Life at the Center

derly persons, each of whom belongs to a different center in a different part of the country, should prove the point. Centers have a powerful impact on the lives of the elderly and make it possible for old age to be a good time of life, sometimes the best.

Baltimore, Maryland

William Doughaday—Age 80

I was the sales manager for my company, and I had men working in four states. I certainly didn't feel ready to stop working, but we had a compulsory retirement age of seventy, and I decided not to fight it.

In June of the year I retired, I had the misfortune of being in the hospital with a gall bladder operation. While I was in the hospital, I developed a back problem. I went to an orthopedic man who said I had a degenerating spinal disk, so for awhile I was in therapy. After that, I did little except recuperate. I still have a back problem, but as far as the gall bladder thing is concerned, it's all cleared up.

In the next few years, I had two strokes, one of which was not serious. Consequently, I had to move downtown to an apartment building because of the effects of the strokes and my back condition. One day I was sitting in the little courtyard just getting a little sun. There was an Episcopal Church across the street where the Waxter Center was conducting a pilot project. This was before the new center was built. The woman in charge of the center at that particular time was Miss Hopper, the director's assistant. She was getting into her car with her arms full of books and things because she was in the process of moving to the new center. Trying to be a gentleman, I hobbled down to her car and held the door open for her. We introduced ourselves and she said, "Why don't you come down to the center?" I said, "Maybe I will. It's a lot better than sitting around at home looking at four walls." My wife's employed. She's much younger than I am and is at work all day.

At the center, Miss Hopper introduced me to a Miss Schneider, who's a graduate in voice of a music conservatory here in Baltimore. Somehow she found that I had sung on the radio back in the late twenties and thirties and that I had been a church singer in the city of Baltimore for a period of forty-six years. I had stopped singing in the church choir as a paid soloist in 1970, after I had those strokes. I was told to move downtown, and I decided to quit because I was afraid to drive.

Miss Schneider said to me, "You're going to start singing again." I said, "Well, I don't think I am." She said, "I think you are." Then I started to go to some of her classes in choral work, which I love. That's how I became interested in the center. I give Miss Schneider all the credit;

she just has a wonderful personality. After a while, I worked with her continually. In March of last year, the center received a grant from the government, and with that money they made me her assistant. That's the capacity in which I work now — I'm the assistant to the music specialist.

I help sort and distribute the music. I help Miss Schneider arrange programs, and when she finds it impossible to be there I take over the classes. We have a class on Tuesday and one on Wednesday, both composed of elderly people. The one on Tuesday is for persons from day care centers and nursing homes. Some of them are brought in there on wheelchairs. Sometimes I direct and Miss Schneider plays the piano. If she's not there, I play the piano and direct at the same time. On Wednesdays, the class is for our regular choral group.

We perform all the time, going out to different nursing homes around the city or anywhere we can get a bus to take us. We have about forty-five to fifty people in each of these groups, so they're big choruses. Some of them have had church choir experience, but most of them have not. We don't have enough men; we only have six or seven that we can depend on regularly. I like to go out to these nursing homes and sing for the people. First, it makes me feel good inside. Secondly, it makes me feel that I'm doing something worthwhile rather than sitting around at home, looking at four walls.

I had started on a volunteer basis, but when they received the grant, they put me on the payroll for five hours a day, so it's really a part-time job. We have programs everyday at one o'clock, always some sort of musical program. Sometimes when the performers don't show, Miss Schneider calls on me to perform by myself. I am asked to sing a couple of times a year down there. A men's glee club is being formed, and Miss Schneider wants me to direct it. If we can get enough men, we will sing four-part harmony, and that will take a lot of work. Sometimes working with music does create problems because I can't do other things, but my music comes first in my life. It's always been my hobby, and I just love it.

I never feel I'm working too hard because Miss Schneider is very understanding, capable, and musical herself. She knows exactly what my physical condition is, and I get a report from the doctor which I pass on to her.

What I like best about the center, of course, is the music. I don't participate in the other things, but they do a lot of good things down there for people; for instance, they have arts and crafts, and language classes, a pool and physical fitness classes.

Going to the center has brought me out, more so than ever before. I had stopped singing. Now I'm singing and going out and appearing before the public again. It used to be that I didn't do any singing unless I was paid for it. Now I realize there's more to life than expecting something from somebody else. There was an elderly lady at a home where I sang recently. When I finished, she came and patted my arm and said, "Please come back. We don't hear anything like that." Of course, that made me feel good all over. If you had given me a fifty-dollar bill, you couldn't have pleased me more.

I wish that I could have done nothing but sing. I would have done it early in life if I could have afforded it, but I was born and raised on a farm and I only had an eighth-grade education. Boys entered the working world in my time when they graduated from grade school. They went to work, not to high school. When I was seventeen, I went to night school and took a business course for four years. When I got a job on the railroad, I realized that I didn't have enough education, so I went to Johns Hopkins at night for three years and finished my schooling.

But I had always wanted to sing. When I was on the railroad, I joined a choir that won a contest. I was studying voice, and my teacher wanted me to go to Italy. He said, "Go to Italy for two years and I'll put you in the Metropolitan." I told him I couldn't do that because I was married and was buying a home. He said, "If you want to choose music as a career from an operatic standpoint, you have to chuck all that." I told him I wasn't brought up that way, and when you assumed responsibilities you had an obligation to stay with them. So he said he would make me a church singer. That's how I wound up as a soloist in the church.

There are times I regret not going to Italy. When I hear Beverly Sills or some other famous singers, I sometimes wonder whether or not I made a mistake. On the other hand I have two boys, and I wouldn't have had them if I had gone to Italy.

My family is delighted with what I'm doing now. It makes them very happy to see how I've come back after all that illness, and that I am qualified to do a job like this.

Being handicapped, I can't go out and take a regular job. I just don't feel capable. There's stress, and I can't work under stress. I developed

Life at the Center

high blood pressure after four years of being in management, and I've had it ever since. If the center were to close, I guess I would just have to sit around the house.

One of the first things people must realize is that they're going to grow old one day. I made up my mind that I was going to grow old gracefully. That's one reason why I was quite anxious to go to the center when I was invited. I had enough drive within me to become involved in things. I like to be part of the action, not one of those who sits around and listens to what's going on. It's something to develop your mind and keep you going. If it hadn't been for the center, I would have been dead, to put it bluntly. My doctor told me that.

I try to live my life in such a way that when it comes time for me to go, I'll be ready to go. The Bible says that the days of our life are three score and ten. I'm about to become four score years old, but I have no fear of dying. I have lived a good life. I'd hate to leave my family, but that's only normal. I realize the fact that I'm approaching the end of the line, but I'm not ready to get off yet. I'm just not ready to get off.

Durham, North Carolina

James Markham—Age 69

The people at the center are extremely nice — they're very friendly to me. We're all in the same boat. We go to the center for a definite reason — to enjoy the companionship we find there. Even if some of the people aren't as alert and strong as the others, I think they can still learn something and feel better, or they wouldn't come. I don't believe that people get up, and dress up, put on their good clothes and go to the center to sit as a child would in a playpen. They go there for a definite reason — to feel better. That's why I go.

I'm sixty-nine. I worked until January 1, 1974. I was sixty-five in July and retired at the end of the year. I had worked at that job for fourteen years. Prior to that I was self-employed. It was a forced retirement. I did not want to retire. When I received a letter from the main office, I contacted my immediate superior. He asked me if I wanted to retire. I said, No. He said, "You can't afford it, can you?" I said, "No, I can't." He said he knew he couldn't afford it either. He said, "Let me have the letter," and he took it to the main office. The reply was that I and several others must retire, that this was company policy, which we had not known. It upset me to a degree, because I was financially not ready for it. I'd been able to perform my duties as well at retirement as at any time in my employment.

When I retired I had plans to do supplementary work, and with my Social Security and my wife's Security, we were hoping to be able to live on it. I was also hoping to work each year to supplement that as much as I could. I was a legatee in a will; I took the money and bought a house on account of my wife, and had only lived here six months when she died. I still live in the house.

About eighteen months ago, when I lost my wife, I went through a long time of terrible depression. I went to a private psychiatrist. He said in his experience the hardest problem he had in dealing with older people was depression and loneliness. And that for me to come to him would take a long time and be very expensive. I told him what my resources were, and that I wouldn't be able to afford his services. He recommended that I join the OARS program at Duke — Older Americans Resources and Service Center, which is psychiatric and medical. OARS recommended I go to the

Life at the Center

senior citizens' center, and I attended it the other four days a week, which has provided an outlet for some of my time, which I've enjoyed very much.

When I went into this depression I thought I was washed up. After forty-four years of marriage, it hit me almost like death itself. I'd never done any housekeeping or cooking. My wife had always attended to that sort of thing. We'd had a rather large family. Now I'm cooking my breakfast. I'm not a good housekeeper and I'm not a good cook. I don't like it. My biggest problem is the loneliness. The days I go to the senior center, I do have people to eat with. If I can, I go out with someone to eat; otherwise I eat alone and spend the evening by myself. I do not enjoy that particularly. My eyesight isn't too good; I can't read for a long time. And TV is so rotten. The new relationships and friendships I've made through the senior center have greatly alleviated this loneliness. It's the biggest part of my life. I spend an average of four hours a day there, all the time it's open, from about 10:00 to 2:00. I have a son who has a business, and I finish up my afternoons there.

At the center I usually play cards. We have a devotional group once a week, a singing group once a week, ceramics once a week. I think the program could be improved. A group of us made up a list of suggestions. Our program director told me we don't have some of these things because the coordination council is out of money. We don't have crafts anymore, and the ceramic program is almost at a standstill because we don't have any equipment. The lady who directs that has to take part of the work home and do it herself, bringing it back and forth.

I get along with everyone there. They are all very friendly. I haven't had any problems at all. In our group we have a daily average of around forty or fifty. We had a birthday luncheon — we have one a month — and we had eighty people then.

I've also been dating one of the ladies for the past three or four months, which I've enjoyed very much. We haven't gotten that far along yet, but I think some body of people, some people with political influence, should be able to change the Social Security laws that require in the marriage of two retired people, that one of them has to give up his Social Security, which makes it impossible for them to live. It would open the door for much more happiness for people over sixty-five who are missing that on that account. There are those of us who think it's morally wrong for an older man and woman to live together unmarried in order to retain their Social Security. That's how I feel, too.

I was hoping to get married, frankly, but this financial thing has got me in a bind. My children think it's a good idea if it would make me happier. Just because you're older and retired, this doesn't keep you from needing to love and be loved by the opposite sex. I don't see why with the right person you can't find the last years as good as you did the first years of your married life.

I don't know what I would have done if there hadn't been a center — what alternative I would have had. I would have kept searching. One thing I kept doing was going to church. I have always believed in it; I raised my family to go to church. I had a problem with alcoholism; that was several years ago. I went to Alcoholics Anonymous. In that program a very big thing is spiritual recovery. Alcoholism is a very difficult problem. I believe nobody can fully recover from it without a spiritual awakening. I've heard a lot of preachers say they couldn't do the whole job, and the psychiatrists say they couldn't do the whole job and the medical doctors say they couldn't do the whole job. It takes a combination of all of it to make a complete recovery. I still attend meetings and I went to the state convention.

My spiritual life changed considerably, thanks to the psychiatric help I got, plus the counseling I had in OARS; all of it helped me snap out of my depression. I was raised in a Southern Baptist home. I had always seen God as a God of fear, not a God of love. Now that's changed; I can feel conscious contact with Him. That has helped me a lot. This was both a result of experience and a conscious decision to change my ideas.

My new attitude toward God has made the world feel more a loving place. My friends tell me they can see a tremendous change in me in the past year, in my attitude. When I was depressed I was ready to call it quits; I had no purpose for living. Now I'm going to make the best of it. There's bound to be something good down the road, I feel. But when I was depressed I had given up; I couldn't see anything good happening. I had no intention of marrying again, or anything.

I get along very well with all of my children. I have five children altogether. Two children live in Durham, one in Florida, one in Atlanta, one in Lumberton, North Carolina. I have ten grandchildren. Little children get on my nerves after a while. I'm not a good baby sitter . . . I go out quite often with my son and his wife who live here and enjoy the things they enjoy. We go out to eat. We have pig pickins — that's when you cook a pig and pick him up over the open barbeque. We did that last New Year's Eve. I enjoy sports; all my boys were athletes. I still enjoy that a lot. I follow it. Football, basketball are very good in this area. My older son went to State College. Two boys of mine had football scholarships in

Life at the Center

college. So I followed it all through junior, senior high, through college. I watch it on TV. I kind of pull for the Redskins.

I get kidded about being over the river, being old, but I take it lightly. I've never felt any ridicule from younger people. I think younger people now have an entirely different conception of older people than what I had. In my time, they always lived with the younger children. Now that's very rare. Now the older person lives by himself or has a companion he lives with. In my own particular case I had a grandmother and grandfather who lived with us until they died. That sort of thing is rare now. So that gives younger people a different conception of older people. I believe they think there is a gap there, but it's no wider than it used to be. I believe older people have more respect from younger people than they used to.

I think the advantage of being old is the experience you have. I knew a man who built a business that made him a millionaire, not on the basis of education, but of experience. There is no replacement for experience, not knowledge or anything. Nothing can replace it in certain areas. People who have worked thirty or forty years are more dependable; they have more interest in their jobs. My son finds older women to be the most dependable employees he can have.

I've never been dependent on my children financially, and I hope I never will be. I hope to be able to work some a little later. My health isn't such that I can do manual work, but I can do supervisory work. I'd look for a managerial-type job, part time, but I intend to keep going to the center.

We discussed death in our group. We talked about the right to die. There were some differences of opinion, but it was all explained to these people who had thought of it only from one angle, that it is the thing to do. A person, a family, has the right if someone is going to be a vegetable for a time, not to keep him alive by artificial means, just to let him die. I think the group agreed rather unanimously that that was the thing to do. I'm not afraid of death. I think this life is a preparation for another, and when my time comes, I'm going. Meanwhile I'm going to try to get the most out of life.

New York, New York

Frieda Sousa—Age 73

My husband retired from Gimbel's department store when he was sixty-seven and I was sixty. At the time we were living in a tenement apartment on East Tenth Street. I said to him, "We're getting older. We can't keep walking up and down five flights of stairs and we can't afford a high rent." I made out an application for city housing and we were accepted. That's how we came to live in this neighborhood in 1967.

When we moved here, I felt homesick for the old neighborhood. Although lots of my friends had moved or passed away, at least I knew some of the people there. When I came here, I didn't know a soul, not even a store. It was strange. I remember crying for the first two days because I didn't like the rooms. All I liked were the comforts: the incinerator, the elevator, the trees and benches.

I used to see the sign here for the senior center, the Good Companions. But I always walked by because someone told me it was only for Jewish people. I didn't go down until about four years later, when I found out more about it.

Long before I joined the club, my husband and I did some exploring in order to get acquainted with the neighborhood. We spent a lot of time by the East River, which was still very beautiful. We used to take our lunch there. Our children came to see us more often then, and we would go to see them more often, too. We were younger and it was easier to travel.

I read a lot, sometimes trashy things, some times more educated things. I never joined the library, but we have books here. My children always brought books home and I read them. I read Dreiser and Hemingway and other people. I kept busy, but just reading books and going down to the East River and holding hands with my husband weren't enough. I knew I wasn't satisfied, but I didn't know what I wanted to do.

I spent a lot of time alone. I didn't make friends easily. Somehow the women weren't exactly my type, so I didn't quite fit in. I was always friendly and talked to them, but not intimately. In fact, it took me four years to really get acquainted here. When I got to know the people who went down to the center, several of them said to me, "Why don't you come down?" I said, "I don't think I belong there." They said, "Of course you

Life at the Center

do." I thought about it. The person who had told me that only Jewish people could go to the center wasn't exactly a friend; she was a neighbor who happened to live next door. When I had said I was thinking about going down, she said very plainly, "You can't because you're not Jewish." Later, I realized she was wrong, because I met some Spanish people who went there.

In the summer, I always saw the center members coming back from trips. They told us about the places they had gone to and I knew I wanted to go on the trips that they took to the state parks and beaches. One day I made up my mind and said to my husband, "Let's go down and join the center. We can play Bingo there." I went and said I would like to register. At that time you had to pay $2.00 in dues. My husband joined, too.

I remember my first day there. Someone said, "You're in a lot of trouble; you're not allowed to play Bingo." I showed him my membership card and he was kind of embarrassed. Instead of getting angry, I smiled and he smiled back. Right away the people liked me because I didn't argue. The same day, I got a note from another table that said, "What's your name?" I answered and she wrote back, "I'd like to get to know you better." That felt good.

I met the staff. Emma was the arts and crafts person and I started to do little things with her: ceramics, glass and painting. When I started painting, I knew nothing about mixing paint or anything. I had never done anything artistic before, except knitting and crocheting which I had learned in Europe.

Gradually I started to do more things. I began to play cards. I joined the chorus. All of this was very good for me. Later there were other important changes. Mostly I learned about working with people. I even went to college for that. The center made it possible for me to take up social work at NYU for sixteen weeks. I got one certificate, and then I went back to leadership school and got another certificate.

It's funny. I'm doing things I never did before, using abilities I didn't even know I had, and yet all these things came about so naturally. The director helped me by giving me confidence and pushing me here and there. If somebody believes you can do something, you stand up to the challenge. After about a year, I was appointed to the advisory board of the center. That's the elected group of members which makes recommendations to the director about the center and the way it's run.

Years ago, I belonged to the PTA and I took minutes at the meetings, so when the director asked me to do it for the advisory board, I said I would. Then an election for vice-president came up and I got a majority of the votes. Because of the illness of the president, I run the meetings. I can remember having to ask what "agenda" meant. Now I'm responsible for keeping one. I didn't think I'd be able to run the meetings, maintaining order, not letting people interrupt when someone is speaking. I even know a lot of *Robert's Rules*. The director says I'm doing a very good job.

I also belong to the Neighborhood Community Board. I'm the secretary there. Last year I was voted a member of the Board of Directors of Henry Street, which is a big honor. I give reports from these meetings to the advisory board here and keep the two groups in touch. Another big event in my life was being selected as the most outstanding senior citizen from our center. I was presented with a certificate from the borough president. I was even on TV with the City Commissioner on Aging for New York.

The advisory board, the community board, and the board of directors only meet a few times a month, so I have time to do the other things I enjoy. I run a figure-watching class at the center once a week in the morning. I learned that from a staff member who started it here. About a year ago, she left and I took over. I'm active in dramatics and I'm on the grievance committee — the committee that listens to members' complaints and problems. I love to write for the newspaper. I attend meetings and report on them, and I do all kinds of assignments. I'm also a senior volunteer, sending out cards to people who become hospitalized or homebound.

My husband asks me, "If I were as busy as you, who would clean the house?" He does a lot in the house. I come home and cook dinner for him every night. He's on a special diet, and he's not supposed to eat certain foods. I think I can count on my fingers the number of times we went out to dinner, except on vacations.

My husband doesn't participate in any of the activities here except for the summer trips, which he loves. It doesn't make me feel bad that my husband doesn't do these things with me. It pleases me that he's proud of me. He says that I sacrificed so much in my younger years that I should just enjoy what I'm doing now. The good things that have happened to me at Good Companions in the last three years seem like a reward for all the earlier hardships. I remember a time during the Depression when my husband lost his job. It was very hard to get another one. He was out of work for two months. The few dollars we had went very fast — rent, milk for the children, coal. We went to a local grocery store, and even though he didn't know us, the grocer said, "Mrs. Sousa, anything you need for the children, take." He was a really nice person. He was so good to us; I'll never forget him.

It was hard in Europe, too. In the old country — it was Austria then; now it's part of Yugoslavia — we had a farm and we all worked very hard. But my ambition was to leave and to better myself. I wanted to be a teacher. I was the best student in the school. My teachers wanted me to go to Vienna and study. The papers were signed for me to study on a scholarship when the war broke out in 1914.

I came to America in 1921. My second job here was taking care of a little boy for a family in New Jersey. I used to look at the comics in the newspaper and remember how things were spelled. That's how I learned English. I loved to learn and I always had an ambition to learn, but I couldn't go to school when my children were young. I wanted to later, but I wasn't confident enough to try. Now I regret not having gone back to school sooner. When I was younger, my memory was better.

When I first went to college, I felt really scared. Again, I was afraid that I probably wouldn't fit in. But it didn't take me long to feel comfortable. There were other older people there who were also worried. Some of them were very intelligent, and I learned a lot from them. There are still many things I'd like to learn. I'd like to study grammar to improve my writing. I'd like to take a psychology course to find out more about why people do this or don't do that.

There are things about myself I want to improve. I want to meet people, talk to them, not to be timid and to be able to come out with the right words at the right time. Sometimes when I go to a board of directors meeting, I'm afraid to ask questions. They're lawyers and are so well spoken, and I get afraid that I won't say the right thing. On the other hand, I know that everyone makes mistakes — educated people, too.

This isn't a private club; it's funded by the government. If the government says people are entitled to a meal, then they should have it, period. On Sunday, people come in from the Bowery to eat. They're alcoholics, but they're clean and polite. I can't understand why other people don't want them to have their meals here. I've met people who have led different lives than I have, but you find out they're the same. We are children of God and we are all human beings.

I guess loneliness makes people change for the worse. They dream about the things they would like to have happen, and if it doesn't happen, they become very bitter and disillusioned. You have to spend time with others. I've found that the way for me to be happy is to pay attention to other people.

If you don't go down to the center, you begin to neglect yourself. You don't get dressed, and you go around in your slippers and housedress. You don't care if your hair is fixed or combed. Going to the club makes you want to look nice. It makes you satisfied when you look at yourself and say, "I look all right today."

It keeps you young longer when you're involved and active. People always put age and dying together. I don't think about death. It will come, that's all. I don't fear death. The only thing I fear is sickness, being confined in the house, being dependent on other people for help. My husband never talks about dying either. We both have good health. There's a little arthritis, but nothing that really bothers us. The basic things are all right. Our hearts are all right. I'm thankful for that. My mother died in her early sixties, my father at seventy. I used to do farmwork, feeding the pigs. The fact that we had healthy, homegrown food all the time and enough to eat when I was young might be what makes me healthy now.

Right now we have a lot more money than we ever had before. My husband gets Social Security. Even though the children offer, we don't have to take money from them. We can buy presents for them on their birthdays and holidays, which makes us feel good.

My children had a fiftieth wedding anniversary party for us at the center a few years ago. About two hundred people were there. My son made a speech. He said that he and his sisters had the most wonderful childhood they could imagine. I was very proud, of course. They were all smart children and we encouraged them, but they never had luxuries and they grew up understanding that nobody can have everything in life.

They all like to write. I think it runs in the family. I write a lot; not that I can do it so well, but it sounds so nice when I put down something on paper and read it back to myself. I started when my nephew began asking me questions about his mother's life in Europe. I wrote everything down. It's for the grandchildren now. There are so many stories here at the center that someone could write an interesting book about. Who knows, maybe I'll try it sometime.

Every so often I wonder what would have happened to me if we had stayed in the old neighborhood on Tenth Street. What would I be doing today? I think probably I would just be going through the routine of eating, sleeping and reading, without outside interests. For me, going out would have meant going down five flights of stairs, going to the park, going shopping and coming back home. I think if we had stayed at the old house, I really would have felt seventy-three years old, but now I don't. These last four years have been the happiest of my life. The people here like me and respect me and I like and respect them. It's hard to describe the feeling inside. I look at the center like a big family, and everyone means something to me. I feel like I belong to Good Companions and Good Companions belongs to me.

Every day is interesting. There's always something to talk about. We hold our own rap sessions. We talk about what is happening and what we would like to do. I feel important to myself. It's like a new life has begun.

For Art's Sake

Immortality has probably tickled the fancy of humankind from the time its members first became aware that everyone alive had to die, that life did not go on forever. There is a sense though, symbolic if nothing else, in which the great artists escape the ultimate fate, because their works survive past their lifetime. We even call their efforts "creative," which means to bring into existence. And there is something highly dramatic about artists continuing to exercise their creativity even as they come close to the end of their own existence. Like the immortal works that they achieved in their old age, which remain for the world to wonder at and enjoy, the images of these old artists linger in the mind. They themselves have become somewhat wondrous, undeniable proof of the strength and value of old age.

In ancient Greece, Sophocles at the age of eighty-nine, wrote *Oedipus at Colonus,* which ranks not only as one of the greatest dramas about old age ever written, but also as one of the world's greatest dramas. Michelangelo, from the time he passed seventy-five until his death at eighty-nine, with a crippled leg, suffering from gout, failing vision, and what was probably a prostate disorder, achieved some of his finest masterpieces: he designed and painted the dome of St. Peter's, frescoed the walls of the Pauline chapel and sculpted his loveliest *Pietà.* The 19th-century Italian composer, Verdi, wrote two of his most acclaimed operas — *Othello* and *Falstaff* — between the ages of seventy-three and ninety. William Butler Yeats, acknowledged as the supreme Irish poet of this century, wrote ever more brilliantly as he aged and continued to do so until his death at seventy-four. He was blind in one eye and hard of hearing for virtually the last twenty years of his life.

The general assumption is that a decline in creativity goes along with aging, and should physical troubles appear, then the loss will be even greater. There are examples of artists who did not, for one reason or another, continue to be productive in their old age, but many others did.

For Art's Sake

The legendary figures mentioned above are just a few in the history of the arts whose creativity did not fail, but actually gained in energy, brilliance and authority. This fact enables us both to assert the presence of creativity through a lifetime and to bury another bothersome myth.

While the persistence of creativity has rich implications for America's elderly, a vast majority of cultural commissars think not, arguing that older people spend more time watching the Fonz and Bionic Woman than they do at theaters or concert halls. In 1976, of all the elderly, only forty-five percent attended at least one event at some cultural center, which would seem to indicate they are less than devotees of the arts. However, we can find some good reasons for this apparent lack of interest.

First is their limited incomes. The high cost of a ticket to any cultural event sends even a sturdy budget into shock, and must be very discouraging to the majority of the elderly, whose incomes are below lower middle class levels. Accessibility is another problem. Theaters are seldom close to residential areas, so there is often a lack of convenient transportation. Furthermore, the majority of performances are scheduled at times which are prime only for the punk criminals who seek elderly victims. An older person with a minimum of good sense will avoid the lonely walk down dark unprotected streets that coming home from a theater frequently means. Meanwhile, the evidence from senior centers is that whenever tickets to concerts and plays are available for an afternoon at either little or no cost and transportation is provided, the elderly are ready, willing, and eager to join the audience. In view of these facts, the supposition that there is a significant relationship between educational level and involvement with the arts, an idea put forth by some social thinkers who point to the low percentage of high school graduates among the elderly, may not hold up.

But if it has truth, it's most likely due to the complexities of our modern society, which have institutionalized the arts and made them into hothouses, upper-class pleasures with intimidating labels. Until recent years, folk art was important to the lives of the poor, uneducated members of society. Examples of such art are expressive and beautiful: old English ballads, the folk dances of Eastern Europe and our own jazz and bluegrass music. Further, it's worth remembering that Shakespeare's plays were supposed to be as popular among London's lower classes as they were among the nobility. Even today, if one can find a relatively stable population with roots in a place which has not been torn apart by technological improvements, there the people dance and sing in moving, exuberant style. Nor do the older people stay at home when the music starts.

Neither nostalgia for a less alienated time nor much of anything else can turn the clocks back. However, being aware of the conditions that once made it possible to experience the arts as a vital part of living could help us achieve a more dynamic relationship between the arts and the elderly in our time and place. Two keys are familiarity and relevance.

Kenneth Koch understands this. He's one of America's better poets and probably one of our best teachers. In 1976, the Columbia University professor conducted a poetry workshop for twenty-five residents of a nursing home located in a dreary New York City slum neighborhood. The members of the group were painfully crippled, frequently sick and depressed, most in wheelchairs and ranging in age from seventy to ninety. They had been cooks, clerks, porters, domestics — poor people with little education, and less interest in poetry. Koch broke down their sense of poetry as a fancy thing of meters and rhymes, while demonstrating that their own life experiences and perceptions were poetry's substance. He refused to be condescending, to disregard standards of excellence, and this approach led the group to achieve a poetry of astonishingly high quality.

When Koch left the workshop after sixteen weeks, these disabled nursing home residents had gained the realization that they could create something beautiful from within themselves, good poems from the long-neglected details of their own lives, which gave those lives new worth. Other results: the nursing home staff reported that the members of the group were more alert, focused and enthused in their daily behavior than they had been before.

There are many other programs around the country in which the elderly participate in acting, painting, singing, dancing — doing rather than watching. A governmental agency, The National Endownment for The Arts, is the primary funding source for these projects. The National Center on the Arts and Aging, an NCOA program established in 1973, is a resource for both artists and people working in the field of aging, each of whom may be uncertain about the other and how to join forces. It is this alliance of vigorous institutions and the efforts of their able personnel that is creating a remarkable thrust. The ultimate role of the arts in the lives of the elderly is undetermined at present and remains to be explained by the future, when social and esthetic possibilities that are now being touched will be better understood.

As has been mentioned, old artists are nothing new. If we intend to assist the elderly in actively engaging the arts, it would be instructive to turn to those artists who have already grown old in the services of their muse. It's one thing to open the garden gate, another to have turned the soil, planted, weeded and picked the bouquet. Old artists are in one sense what our initiates may become, but those artists who have been around a long time, working creatively in the midst of the world's daily practical demands for many decades, must have a unique quality. What's it like to grow old and still be an artist?

Rochester, New York

Howard Hanson—Age 81

I first became involved in music when I was about seven years old. Grieg and Sibelius were my earliest influences. At that time I wrote a small piece which I have today. I still like it.

My mother was quite musical, and neither of my parents ever stood in the way of my musical career. Whatever I wanted to do was all right with them. First, I went to the Institute of Musical Art, which is now the Juilliard School of Music in New York. From there I went to Northwestern University. In 1921, I won the *Prix de Rome* and spent the next three years at the American Academy in Rome. I came to Rochester in 1924.

For the next forty years, until 1964, I was the director of the Eastman School of Music. Eastman is one of the great music schools of the world. I wasn't upset about retiring from the school — in fact, I set the date myself. I'm still a consultant to the school and I'm available at any time. I really retired this year, at the age of eighty-one, from the University of Rochester. That's the oldest retirement age ever. I'm available to them also for some consulting work.

I'm still composing, having finished my seventh symphony this summer. It had its first performance in August at Interlaken, Michigan by the National Youth Symphony. Two years ago I finished my sixth symphony, and it was performed for the first time at the 125th anniversary of the New York Philharmonic. I manage to keep quite busy!

Composing has always been a struggle for me. Creating is a problem, because it forces one to try the impossible. One always tries to create the most beautiful thing possible, and that imposes obstacles. I think I still struggle in that same way. Composing music, just like writing, is a matter of technique. The same technique that you develop in writing you have to develop in composition — there's great similarity. There are problems of logic, of form and consistency. These problems are always there, and it certainly hasn't gotten any easier for me. I think the principles that I followed sixty years ago are still basically the same today. In that respect, I don't think age has made any difference in my work.

Currently, my schedule is a quiet one. I just work a couple of hours a day now, because at eighty-one, you tire more quickly. I do have a definite time period set aside for work, usually from 3:00 to 6:00 in the afternoon. At 3:00, I go into my study and work, either at the piano or at my desk.

Right now I'm working on a ballet for a very good friend of mine who is the ballet mistress at the school in Chatauqua, New York. I've promised to give her a brand-new work, a ballet in four movements, and I'm quite pleased with the way it is progressing. At first, I was a little worried, because the ballet comes so soon after the completion of the symphony. That work took me about a year and a half to complete, and after finishing such a major piece, I feel rather depleted. It took me about two months to get the battery recharged, but now I'm happy to say I'm operating on all six cells again.

I composed my first symphony in 1921 when I was still in Rome. It was first performed in 1924 by the old New York Symphony under Walter Damrosch. It's an ecstatic feeling to hear your work performed for the first time. Opening night is thrilling, of course, but I think the greatest experience is the first rehearsal. Until then, you've had this work in your mind, but you've never really heard it. Then, for the first time, you can hear what you've created. I still get the same excitement every time I hear a new work of mine being performed. The passage of time hasn't diminished the thrill at all.

Having been at Eastman for so many years, I've had many, many students. Some of them have won Pulitzer Prizes, and some have gone on to become famous composers themselves. The current president of the Juilliard School was a student of mine.

I've been asked advice many times, of course, and I have one important piece of advice for a composer to keep in mind — be yourself. Find out who you are, and stick to your philosophy. Don't be swayed by what the critics think or what the public thinks. This is the primary function of the creative artist, and if you aren't yourself, who are you?

I was never much swayed by what people thought. I was always pretty much my own man, but I think I'm more true to myself now than ever. When you get to be eighty years old, you have the freedom of speaking your own mind. You have nothing to lose anymore and nothing really to gain. I also think a respect for your age develops in people. Sometimes I do get the feeling that I'm being treated as a grand old man of music, but I don't mind that at all. I can't say that age has made me more honest than before, but I do have fewer inhibitions.

I don't quite know what my proudest achievement has been, but I'm probably proudest of all the students who have come through the Eastman School, and all the prizewinners who have come from my classes. It's a great source of pride and delight for me. The greatest personal thrill I've had was the first performance of my opera on the stage of the Metropolitan. That was way back in 1934. I can't describe the thrill of standing on the stage of the Met.

I liked teaching very much. I've always taught and have never felt that teaching got in the way of my own productivity. As a matter of fact, I found that teaching really contributed a lot to my own work. I could see another young composer's problems and relate them to my own work. The fact that I don't have that day-to-day contact now doesn't really have any effect on my own work, though. The big factor now is the matter of physical energy, how much physical and emotional energy I can maintain. I think it takes a little more time to work up steam at eighty than it does at forty.

There's nothing in particular that I haven't done that I still want to do. I've done a lot of guest conducting, leading every major orchestra in the country. People have always asked why I never wanted to go on and become a famous conductor. It's just something that I never wanted to do. There's quite a difference between conducting and composing — it's an entirely different feeling. Composing, after all, is creating. In conducting, you're up there in front of an orchestra. You're the maestro and you're telling everybody what to do. I must say that I prefer the creative end of it. So, for all the thrills that I've gotten from conducting, I compose instead of pursuing a career as a conductor.

But I still do a little bit of conducting. I'll be going out to the University of the Pacific, where I started teaching in 1916, for that purpose. As a conductor, I always choose the material that I'm going to conduct, and being a composer, I enjoy conducting my *own* work most. After that, I'm very fond of the Russian repertory. Russian and French music are my two favorites, although Beethoven is my favorite composer.

There have been tremendous changes in the musical world during my lifetime. America has come of age. Our orchestras are without question among the greatest in the world. Orchestras like Boston, New York, Philadelphia, and Chicago are just unsurpassed. Also, the young American artist has certainly come into his own. I think that, creatively, we've finally begun to arrive. Men like Copeland, Samuel Barber and a number of others are beginning to make an impression, not just on the American scene but internationally as well. This just wasn't true forty years ago.

For Art's Sake

I'm very much interested in new trends in music. Of course, it's very hard to keep up with everything, but I try. Some current things just aren't very good. In the field of popular music, there are some very appealing things and some simply awful things being done. When people ask me my opinion of popular music, I can't really answer. There's no general statement. I don't even know the names of the people I've liked.

Looking back on it all, I feel I've probably followed a rather steady course. There's nothing that I do now that I wouldn't have done twenty years ago. I can't think of anything I would not have done, just maybe some things that I shouldn't have done!

New York, New York

Joseph Konzal—Age 72

I've been an artist off and on for about fifty years. I had to take some time off to make a living, teaching or working in commercial art. I often ask myself why I started sculpting. In high school I did well in art and I always liked working with tools. I came to New York when I was twenty and worked in commercial art studios which I didn't like. I also studied painting and sculpting at the Art Students League. I don't know when I first felt that sculpting was my life's work. It just sort of happened.

The art world is much different now than when I came here from Milwaukee in 1926. It wasn't as extended as it is now. I like the idea that people are working in painting, sculpture and crafts. I think it's good. It's something that takes you back to working with your hands and is just the opposite of push-button work. This is a push-button age now, and things are getting out of hand. New York is an example of that, especially in the rotting-out areas of the South Bronx. I can't understand how it is happening. We can go to the moon and all kinds of fantastic things, but we can't live properly. If you don't have any money, living is tough and the artist can't do anything about it. . . all he can do is bring people back to earth. You can say, "Man does not live by labor alone," but artists really can't change anything.

I've just come back to New York from Kent State, where I taught for five years. I enjoyed my time there, although five years is a long time and I missed New York. I think teaching can be very stimulating, but full-time it's pretty tough. I was retired; that's why I stopped. It takes a lot out of you, though, and I think a lot of people who teach get stuck. There's nothing wrong with that, but you don't get much work done. You have to settle for that.

I was leery about teaching because I had never gone beyond high school. I always had a very dumb notion about teaching: "Those who can't, teach." That's stupid, of course. It depends on your whole makeup. I liked working with the students, both graduates and undergraduates. I was lucky to have some very good students, and I'm still in contact with some of them. The difference in age between them and me makes it difficult to feel like peers, but I get along with them. I told a number of them to come to New York to live. I thought it would be a good place for them to come, not just for a couple of weeks, but for a while. I thought these students had a lot on the ball, but I certainly didn't give anybody any illusions about making it big.

I do miss Kent State, all the activity there. In a way it was kind of a letdown to come back, even though I'm very glad to be back in New York. It's a re-establishing process, but it's also a problem of age, too. Age is not a good thing in this country. I don't know about anywhere else. Friends of mine have gone through it, too. The galleries would prefer young people. Not really young people, but people in their forties and fifties. There's no question about it. It took me a while to realize that, and it was quite a shock. There's a future with younger artists, whereas old people don't have a future. It's not exactly true, but it is kind of obvious. When a person is seventy-five, in five years he'll be eighty, and that's pretty old. I imagine that people do get less active, but if one is interested in his work, not just trying to keep busy, it goes a long way. Look at Picasso; he was in his nineties and still very active.

My style has changed over the years. You don't do the same things all the time. I couldn't have done what I do now when I was younger. I have the same influences that I did before — Matisse, Cézanne, and Rodin — whom I appreciate even more than I did before. I grew and matured. I hope that I'm still growing. I still have to struggle; it's always been a struggle, I think that's true of all artists at all levels. I had periods when I was younger when I couldn't work. When I started teaching part time and had more time, it got easier. I was unhappy when I wasn't working, although it isn't all a bed of roses. I've always enjoyed the arts — sculpture, music, and dance — but I always used to wonder if it was important for me to be doing it. It took a long time before I was convinced that it was important. I also realized that I was a lot more happy getting things done and getting into shows and galleries. Coming to terms with the fact that art is important to me, I think, made work easier for me.

I think I have a fairly good underground reputation. I never really made the big time in the galleries like my friend, David Smith. I had a discussion with a friend of mine about regretting. We decided that we all have to do the best we can, no regrets. It's easier said than done. I would have liked to really be out there, but what am I supposed to do, cry about it? I think I did pretty well, all things considered, and I'm very self-critical. The art world is a sort of rat race, too. There's a certain amount of competition involved. I think I understand that better now, too.

I've just been picked for a commission. That was very nice. The

Joseph Konzal

sealed version of the piece was accepted and now the real version is in the hopper. It's a landscape piece for a federal building, a postal office, I think. It'll be shipped out to Dayton, Ohio. I was paid $17,000 for it, but after all the bills are paid, there won't be too much left. I also had a show in April. I'm going to be in the WPA Artists Show — presenting old work and one new work. And I'll also be the Tenth Street Artists Show in Soho. Tenth Street was a very active cooperative movement that lasted for about seven or eight years and then died out. There were probably about seven to ten galleries that were part of the co-op. Although it was never the hoopla that Soho is now, Tenth Street is kind of legendary. I'm going to have a couple of pieces in that show, too.

I enjoy seeing my work around, and to know that it's appreciated is very satisfying. I think that work itself has kept me in good health. People who are retired sometimes feel lost. Health is really the big factor. I exercise, do yoga and stretching exercises. I'm also pretty careful about what I eat. I can imagine retiring and I don't like the idea. I'll worry about it when I'm there. I currently work about thirty to forty hours in my studio. I live nearby and just walk over here and spend the day. As long as I can keep my studio, I'll work there.

I like having a career to look back on. I have two works with me that are kind of special to me that were done between 1963 and '65, wall reliefs. They were part of the work that I got a fellowship for. That in itself doesn't make them special, but looking at them I think they've lasted. They're still very effective and they still interest me. I can look back and say that there were some periods when my powers were their greatest. Even at Kent State, when I was so busy, I had the pep to get a lot of big things done. There's one big steel piece that I really like from that period.

Like everybody else, I don't like the idea of dying. But I realize that an awful lot of people have died and will continue to. I don't put much stock in the immortality of my art. Eventually everything will change. Even the sun is dying. The earth will die, too. It's all a very tricky thing.

Even though you don't want to die, you will. So you make the most of it while you're living. You live a life, a full life, and die happy. Isn't that what it's all about?

San Francisco, California

Ruth Bernhard—Age 72

I just celebrated my seventy-second birthday and my fiftieth anniversary in the United States of America. My family were artists, and naturally I was influenced by my environment. I started photographing around 1930 and have been supporting myself with it all these many years. I had no intention of becoming a photographer, as I was leaning heavily toward music. It was just one of those lucky happenings. Anything related to the arts was a "natural" for me. Since my early childhood I had been eager to go to museums, attend concerts and lectures, anything, just as long as it had to do with the arts.

In 1935 I met Edward Weston, saw his work and was profoundly moved. I had never thought of photography as a medium of art until I had experienced his work. It changed my life. My first creative work after moving from New York to Southern California involved dolls and puppets because some of my new contacts were puppeteers. One of my best known images today is that of a doll's head.

I continued to make my livelihood by working for craftspeople, jewelers, potters, weavers, as well as doing portrait photography, primarily with children. There is hardly anything I can think of which does not interest me, even if I do not choose it as a photographic subject. Sometimes I get hooked on one idea and continue concentrating on it for a long time. Seashells fascinated me for the better part of one year. Although I am deeply interested in the state of the world, I never intentionally express my concerns in my work. Others, however, seem to find them there.

Right now I am organizing my archives, a big job for someone who does not keep notes or dates! Recently I finished thirty portfolios—a much bigger task than I had anticipated. In 1977 I had several overlapping shows, among them the Witkin in New York and Photo Album in Los Angeles. That's a lot of printing in the darkroom.

In 1953 I moved from Hollywood to San Francisco and have thoroughly enjoyed living in the same Victorian flat ever since. I made a lot of new friends and became acquainted with many of my West Coast colleagues. I got to know Imogen Cunningham, Ansel Adams, Dorothea Lange, Wynn

Ruth Bernhard

Bullock, along with many others not so famous but delightful to know. I was closest, however, with Edward Weston and Wynn Bullock.

I don't really think of myself as the Dean of American Photographers; there are many others. When Imogen died, I may have been moving toward that space. But to think that I might even be considered in that vein makes me smile, as no one has ever mentioned this idea to me. It amuses me because I feel so ageless.

The art world is my first interest. When I open the paper, I inform myself about the theater, dance, the galleries and music. There just isn't enough time to see and do it all. Every summer I have been teaching a small group of students in Wisconsin; Minneapolis, Minnesota; Sun Valley, Idaho, and at the University of Logan (Utah). It's always stimulating to meet with such a variety of people.

I hope some day to visit Japan—a trip I've been dreaming of for many years. There's something there that calls to me—the poetry, the crafts, everything!

Not only has the art world changed, but much of our world as a whole seems to have changed. I'm afraid that I'm pessimistic about the future of the human race. All of the arts are naturally responding to our cultural degradation; the arts always mirror the state we are in. There seems to be a lot of meaningless work around. The trend of the time is to imitate those who are successful, to do the fashionable thing; to work from the outside in, rather than from the inside out. To be a creative person is a big responsibility, hard to live up to. One must ask himself, "What must I do to be the best I can be?"

Naturally I have struggled. I did not go to school to learn my trade. I just learned by the doing-failing-and-try-again method. My first job in 1929 in New York was as an assistant to an assistant on a magazine which had its own photo studio. I had learned to set up the 8 x 10 studio camera on the tripod, and barely learned to develop and print, when I was fired. So I bought my own camera, made my first independent photograph of "Lifesavers" candy, and it was also the first of my works to be published in *Advertising Arts* magazine. That was the beginning. Now each of my images is the result of a compelling impulse which I cannot deny. My life and work are one. I think now much more in terms of future images, even in those periods when I'm not actually making new exposures.

Black and white imagery is my form of expression—a very exciting experience, indeed. My photographs come to me in much the same way that I imagine a poem is born. The image is suddenly there. It makes itself known, so to speak, but needs to be refined, simplified, clarified. That process might take the longest time, through the magic of the ephemeral light. The object in front of my camera is transformed in some mysterious way into a new vision.

I demand a great deal of myself, sometimes more than I can produce, but that's the only way I can live with myself. To be a "perfectionist" without ever reaching perfection—that's always a disappointment!

I don't feel that I will be immortalized through my work. To me immortality is the influence and sharing we have passed on to those who come after us, whether it be good or bad, positive or negative. Wondering if my work will prove immortal really is of no great interest to me. I'm very pleased, of course, to have my work in the photographic archives. It's a marvelous solution to a puzzle: What to do with all those prints and negatives accumulated over many years. Whenever I threatened to throw everything overboard, I heard cries of "Oh, no, don't do that!"

My feeling each time I take a photograph is that I celebrate the life I love, and the beauty I know, and the happiness I have experienced. I share this with those who can enjoy it.

I think that life, everything, is recycling. Whatever I have lived and whatever I am, will be recycled. Death is a part of life, a perfectly normal transition. I have no worries or fears about it. I'm in pretty good health and hope to be independent as long as possible and not become a burden to anyone. I just live a normal, active, vigorous life. But when death takes me—that's the right time!

I have been teaching for many years and still do. Photographers visit me a lot. They love to discuss their work and want to know what I think of it. Although I never discourage anyone, I must give them my honest opinion in relation to their talent and future plans.

If I don't see a big enough talent, I might encourage them to use photography as their personal expression and find their livelihood in another field. It seems most unfair, I feel, that art schools and colleges have not made photography students aware of the very limited opportunities available for making a living from photography. The field is so overcrowded, even for the most competent.   •

Ruth Bernhard

I enjoy teaching. I wouldn't do it if I didn't like it. I take it very seriously. I think of a teacher as a gardener, a cultivator, not a destroyer. My special interests are the advanced students. Lately, I have cut down on my classes, at least at the University of California Extension, San Francisco. It took up too much of my time, although I must say I do miss it. Now I have only a few private classes and single lectures.

Most of my friends are young. I enjoy the contact with some of my colleagues, but my closest friends are definitely of this generation, between the ages of thirty and forty, primarily my current students or past students with whom I have developed a constant relationship. We get together socially for lectures, films and dinner.

For pure relaxation, I love reading, listening to music, both classical and jazz. I'm an avid collector of shells, pebbles, feathers, birds' nests. You name it—I collect it. Oh, yes, naturally you can find me at lectures on a variety of subjects.

To be an artist is a great privilege and also a great responsibility. To be allowed to do what you most want to do, in fact to be driven to do it, I consider the greatest gift.

My age has not changed my personality. Sometimes I come across articles written about me in the late forties, and I still feel exactly the same way. I still have the curiosity I was born with, find life utterly surprising. Maybe I realize more all the time how incredible reality is. I'm still looking at the world with wonder. That's why I'm a photographer. I try to look deeply into the puzzle of our existence and find it more fascinating all the time. Perhaps it is only natural for the young to feel they have a monopoly on the lust for life. I notice very little difference in my approach to life and work. The young spirit in me refuses to die. In some ways, I even see improvements. Disappointments do not throw me. I can cope, take things in my stride. Nor do I look back. Today is the time to live to the fullest. At seventy-two, that's progress, isn't it?

Of course, I have my own darkroom, as well as a studio separate from my home. I'm not a bit systematic or compulsive about a daily routine. In fact, I'm not at all well organized. Sometimes I may spend hours printing in the darkroom, or maybe reading or socializing. I indulge myself in my many and varied interests. I'm my own most lenient boss!

To make a photograph is always a very personal, thrilling experience,

For Art's Sake

just for my own pleasure. The thought of a later audience never occurs to me. Lately my prints have been selling well at the galleries and naturally this pleases me. It's an extra dividend to have your work appreciated.

Thinking back on my life, I can't say I have many regrets. I could not have designed a more satisfying life for myself. Living is meaningful, like a great love affair, serious and joyful!

Sherman, Connecticut

Peter Blume—Age 72

I lived in the East New York section of Brooklyn when I was a child. At the age of twelve I started going to an art school which was part of an evening high school. The school was run by a commercial artist; it was very casual. I didn't have a very high regard for any of this, but it got me started.

The atmosphere of an art school is very conducive to serious pursuit. You find people around with great enthusiasm, and you develop contacts. Although it was all oriented to commercial art, I did get something from it. There was an atmosphere of learning there and a kind of determination to succeed and excel, which was quite important. Then I started to work very seriously. Wanting to become an artist as quickly as possible, I thought that going to school would be a colossal waste of time.

By then I realized that my parents were not enthusiastic about my passion for art. They felt it would lead to a very uncertain future. Although we were very poor, any sacrifice would have been fine if I were to be a doctor, lawyer or some sort of decent professional man. But art just seemed to them a terribly risky business. They adjusted finally when I was on my own. My determination was such that neither they nor anyone else could have dealt with it.

I got my first job when I graduated from grade school at about thirteen and a half in a lithographic house, but I had to go back to school until I was fourteen. As soon as I got my working papers, I got a job as a "jack-of-all-trades," doing lithography, engraving and related work.

When I was fifteen, I studied art at the Educational Alliance, a school with a great reputation at that time. It really changed the course of my life. I gave up the idea of becoming a commercial artist. My colleagues at the art school were the Soyer brothers, Chiam Gross and a number of others who have become quite well-known artists. This atmosphere of seriousness and devotion was quite different from anything I had known before. I continued to study there until I was about eighteen, but I was never a full-time student.

By this time I had started painting seriously, so I established a completely different routine. I managed to take in a morning class and work for

For Art's Sake

perhaps four hours or so at the engraving house in the afternoon. Then I would go to another art class in another school where there was a sketch class in which I could work from the models. In the evening I attended another class at the Educational Alliance. Although this schedule sounds a bit hectic, there was nothing extraordinary about it; it was fairly typical.

When I reached eighteen years of age, I realized I had to become a professional. I shared a studio with another student I knew and I started painting. When I had completed two or three paintings that I thought were good, I took them to the Daniel Gallery, one of the more avant-garde galleries of that time. The directors looked at them and encouraged me, asking me to let them look at the next work I did. I did a couple of small paintings, and Mr. Daniel said, "Did you ever think of selling these things?" I hesitated because I didn't really want to sell my paintings. I was making quite a lot of money for someone my age when I worked, which was as little as possible. But I said, "Yes." It wasn't a very large sum for these small paintings, about $150 for the two of them. He immediately turned around and sold them to a collector, and these paintings, done when I was nineteen years old, are now in the Columbus Museum.

After I first left art school, I actually didn't do a whole lot of painting, but instead just thought about things a great deal. When I did start painting again, I became a cubist — a complete departure from anything that I had done in art school or in the Soyers' circle. This change in style represented a whole re-orientation of my life.

My interests were not in Picasso's type of cubism — the things that were done early, before World War I. They were a sort of outgrowth of the things that Delaunay and Ozenfant were creating in France, called "Purism." It appealed to me very much; there was something about the pattern of it that fit into my philosophical thinking at the time, as I was also doing work in that style. I didn't feel that I was motivated to outrage people. I had been working toward what is called Surrealism. I had read the Surrealist Manifesto when it appeared in 1926, and although much of it seemed pretentious and irrelevant, I found some ideas interesting.

I eventually changed to landscapes because I felt an artist had to go through an organic development. Ultimately, I wanted to paint a picture which conveyed a positive meaning to anybody who looked at it, but at first my work seemed rather esoteric. The results rather shocked people. As time went on, I wanted to assimilate a great deal more of the symbolic

Peter Blume

aspects of what goes into a picture and the way in which they are assembled.

I went to Italy on a Guggenheim in 1932. I had just finished the *Light of the World* and from the *Light of the World* I went on to do *The Eternal City*. There was really a progression of certain ideas that led up to this work in an odd sort of way. The articulation and juxtaposition of forms are not outlandish, although some people think they are. It seems like a perfectly natural picture to me.

Over the long period of time that I worked on *The Eternal City*, I never lost the thread of it. I started in the lower right-hand corner and developed the whole thing piece by piece over a period of three years. I never went back and changed a thing. When I went to Italy, I hadn't planned to come back with the idea for painting *The Eternal City* — I just came upon it. Here was Mussolini's great celebration of the tenth anniversary of the March on Rome. It was everywhere — omnipresent. At Exposition Hall in Rome there was a big show of all the martyrs of Fascism, and it was dominated by this very big papier-mâché head of Mussolini. I went all over Italy to places I wanted to see, but the background for all this was Fascism and this great display that the Fascists put on. I spoke for a long time about elements in the painting for the curators at the Museum of Modern Art, and I explained how this idea came to me.

I was walking around the Forum, standing on a parapet that looks down over the old Forum. In the late afternoon light I saw the whole thing quite clearly, *The Eternal City*. I started doing the sketches. One of the shrines is actually in Florence. Hawthorne had described this shrine exactly as I saw it, in writing of his travels through Italy. That big head of Mussolini, of course, became the jack-in-the-box. That wonderful light over the Forum precipitated the idea.

Ideas still come to me like that sometimes. You always wonder how a thing like that happens. You can't make it happen, but certain things acted as catalysts. The ideas suddenly come down like a fluttering bird, and there it is — an idea that's almost fully grown. You might expose yourself to fresh and moving experiences, but you can't create ideas from nothing. The central form of what I've been doing has been based on that principle of painting from a vivid experience.

I recently became involved in sculpture, and I've had a show of my bronzes. When I was young, I studied sculpture at the Beaux Arts Institute

For Art's Sake

of Design. I did modeling at the Beaux Arts for about three or four months, but I went back to painting and didn't do anything in sculpture until about four years ago. In the wintertime when the light failed at 4:30 and I still had a little bit of pep left over, I started making little abstract shapes from little squeezes of wax, putting them all together and shaping them out. Then I found I could carry it a little bit further and began putting things together more seriously. I was interested in Venus and decided to do a whole series on her adventures. I did a lot of reading on the subject before I did the series. It was very gratifying and different from painting.

In doing sculpture you have to realize that there is no illusion — you're working on the real thing. I realized that painting has limitations that sculpture doesn't have. I became interested in the human gesture, and sculpture was the way to express this. I was working in wax, and I learned to make my own armatures. I finally ended up with six pieces in the Venus series, six major ones, half life-size, and quite a number of smaller sizes.

I started out quite systematically, making drawings. I made small models in wax before making the large ones. I had everything wired — all the locks of hair, all the fingers, and all the toes. I was in complete control of the gesture I wanted. I completed the whole series over a period of nine months.

I could never paint a picture like *The Eternal City* again. Why should I? There are things that one does at one stage of life that he never does again. It has nothing to do with evaluating its quality, but with age he does things and sees things in a different way. The results might be better or worse, but he does it anyway. Very often the change in your perception is not immediately apparent, much like the changing aspects of a picture. Each time you see it, it's not quite the same picture you saw before. These things happen imperceptably. The changes do not occur suddenly at the age of sixty-five. You might arbitrarily say, ''Now I'm sixty-five and I won't be doing this or that. I'll never be getting into a situation like that again at my age.'' But no one can be sure; since not all situations can be controlled.

I haven't had a crucial test of aging. The only problem I've had to face because of age is a change in my eyesight. One of the most extraordinary and poignant crises in my career took place when I suddenly realized my eyes, which had been excellent, were middle-aged eyes. I hadn't needed glasses, even for reading, until my mid-fifties. It didn't bother me too much, because I could still paint without glasses. Then I found that as my eyes deteriorated while in my sixties, I had to use glasses for working. I couldn't abide that; it was repugnant. Arm and eye coordination is so exact, because of lifelong experience. With glasses that magnify, a sense of distance is lost. Compensations are made, but the initial shock of the magnification is quite upsetting. At least I found it so. I think it's generally true of painters, who go through a crisis when their eyes change. This must have been true of Titian, who lived until he was ninety-nine. He had to put long extension cords on his brushes so he could focus. Every painter changes as he grows older. There's a tremendous difference between the early Titians and the very late ones.

I keep painting because I've been doing it all my life. There are things in painting that I still want to do, and I don't know if anybody else has done them. I'll go on while I still can. I don't know what my life will be like in my seventies, if I'll find myself weakened by the passage of time. I don't feel weakened now, so I'll just go on. I will probably be painting, but I may be doing something else.

I work all day long. I start in the morning, about 9:00 or 9:30 and I work until a little before 1:00. Then I have lunch. My only change in routine, probably brought on by old age, is a little nap after lunch for about three-quarters of an hour. I nap right in my studio and then go back to what I was doing before lunch. I stop about 4:30 or five o'clock, depending on the light. I guess I work about six hours a day.

I'm not the oldest artist, by any means. I'm no dean of anything. I feel less pressured and I imagine it's another aspect of advancing years. I don't care how much time I waste in the studio. I consider that to be the destructive part of construction. They're related each to the other, because you have to be able to do both. I can tear things up or scratch things out or paint things over. I feel that's the healthy and the proper vigorous attitude to take when you're in the studio. I do think about time, and there are a lot of extraneous things I'm trying to cut out altogether, although I still do everything I can. I like to do physical exercise outdoors and look after my place, mowing and pruning. I'm in pretty good shape at the age of seventy-one.

I've abandoned trying to keep up with new trends. There hasn't been much that's new, just more like a merry-go-round than new movements in art. There have been new variations, of course. In the last twenty years, the arts in America have appeared to express ideas we've seen before, so I don't feel that I'm incapable of understanding them. I think I know exactly what's going on.

One is often not concious of events as they occur, but they do have an effect. One thinks one is exactly the same as when one was twenty, but obviously one is not. I hope I haven't become more conservative; the range of my interests has become much broader.

I just want to go on working peacefully, not in a really quiet way, but just doing exactly what I want. I love to travel, usually between projects. When I travel, I try to expose myself to brand-new experiences. From these can come anything, a surprise. If I can continue to renew myself this way, then I can go on forever. I never think about dying, really. I still think that I'm going to go on and on.

Taking a Chance on Love Again

In the shaping of contemporary American spirit, an odd twisting of life and its purposes has led to a very dangerous Ageist myth. We seem to deny that life ends, and affirm sex as life's purpose. Boil and bubble, this double trouble and the myth emerges: age equals impotence. It's hard for an older person not to worry about that one.

When sexuality is threatened, the ego suffers a heavy shock, which affects both mind and body adversely. And, unfortunately, predictions of imminent impotence for aging men frequently cause that very problem, with subsequent deep depression. Too many elderly persons are victims of a sensitivity to whatever public opinion passes around as truth, even though it's far from reality.

The fact is that sexual ability does not disappear at the age of retirement, or at any particular age. The capacity to perform sexually and enjoy it will last throughout life unless some major illness occurs, or one believes the impotence myth and succumbs to it. But being a matter of mind over myth, this condition can be reversed by sympathetic counseling or psychotherapy.

There are some physical changes that come with aging which require an adjustment of expectations, but they are far from being signals of sexual apocalypse. For males, the frequency of erection and ejaculation diminishes with age. Nevertheless, pleasure doesn't. In some ways it is enhanced; intercourse lasts longer, which can provide more gratification for both partners. Also, testimony from some elderly people indicates that with this extended time has come a heightened appreciation of the sensuality of sex.

The sexual functioning of older women is minimally affected, contrary to folk tales about the perils of menopause. As women age, there is some loss in vaginal lubricity and it takes a longer time for lubrication to happen. While these symptoms, if misunderstood, can result in some

155

Taking a Chance on Love Again

discomfort during intercourse, a little patience (as recommended for the man's longer time for erection) will lead to happier experiences. Further, those difficulties tend to occur less among women who have had and continue to have active sex lives. Disuse is misuse. In any event, those changes that do come to pass do not have an effect on the ability to experience orgasm. In fact, some women report that they have had orgasms for the first time since becoming older. Probably the advent of menopause brings an ease of mind that enables pleasure to flow as it should.

The myth that age equals impotence has plenty of cultural support. Check any of the popular arts for the last 2,000 years — one would be hard pressed to find in them older people taken seriously as lovers. Whenever the theme is considered, the treatment is strictly for laughs, the very idea a big joke. This is the expression of our failure to understand that an older person can have strong sexual feelings and feel deeply for another. We assume that vigorous sexuality, the fuel for romance and love, ends with youth.

Our daily language, too, says so contemptuously. An older man with an observable sexual appetite is spoken of as "a dirty old man," "an old lecher," or "an old goat"; and an older woman is said to be "indecent," a "pathetic old bag," or even "crazy." However, for younger people, any evidence of sexuality short of perversion or blatent pornography is a big plus.

It is as though the chains around human sexuality have been loosened solely for swinging singles and their married friends, while the elderly remain bound in an updated version of 19th-century repression. But despite prevalent asexual images of the elderly as mellow grandpas and kindly grandmas dozing off, each indifferent to the other's sexual indifference, elderly people are very much aware of their sexuality. They value it and are perhaps even more sensitive to its qualities of physical and emotional intimacy than younger people, for whom sex is often a way of making their way in the world.

With daily work and the concerns of raising a family mainly a part of their past, the elderly have more time to be with people, with friends and loved ones. There tends to be a greater emphasis on personal relationships and on emotional needs. The awareness that time is running short makes keener the urge to be intimate with a loved spouse. The feelings of belonging and trust, the release in expressing oneself and having feelings responded to and shared, the warm comfort of bodily closeness, the pleasure of giving pleasure and the joy of the sexual embrace have a primacy that life's earlier circumstances may never have allowed.

Yet fifty-three percent of the elderly who are widows and twenty-one percent who are widowers no longer experience that intimacy. It is not easy to recover from the loss of someone with whom one has shared more than

Taking a Chance on Love Again

half a lifetime; nor is it easy to begin anew with someone else. The prospect does not appeal to many elderly widows and widowers, who resign themselves to being alone. For those who never enjoyed being married, aloneness may offer possibilities for self-discovery or bring welcome relief. But there are other elderly people who, having grieved for their deceased spouses and who have refused to abandon their need to love and be loved, remarry.

Not much research has been done on people who've remarried after age sixty-five. There are no figures on how many there are, or who they are. We do know that in one year, 1973, according to data received by the U.S. Department of Health, Education, and Welfare, there were at least 16,407 brides and 33,020 grooms over sixty-five. All but five percent of this group had been previously married. The difference in numbers between the men and women who remarried is not so much a comment on the relative inner resiliency of the two sexes as it is on what society approves. Older men are regarded as good choices for younger women, and the figures indicate that the grooms chose accordingly. Unfortunately, society does not offer older women an equal opportunity, and their chances for remarriage are sadly limited.

Among those elderly persons who remarry, the probability is that most would refer to their previous marriage or marriages as happy. They have known the deep satisfactions of physical and emotional love and realize the impoverishment of life without them. They are confident of being able to live lovingly and get along with another person. There are also men and women who had miserable marital experiences, some more than once. Yet they feel that they've learned from their mistakes and having fallen in love, remarry and find happiness.

Of course, not all of the elderly who remarry are swept away by high tides of love. Some are prompted by excessive dependency needs and reenter matrimony with little thought of who and why. Others do it in cool calculation for money or status. Whatever the wrong reason, they will suffer the troubles that a loveless marriage brings, regardless of age.

By their action, those elderly people who marry for the best of reasons — love — jostle several assumptions about the diminished, nonassertive nature of aging. Frequently they have to ignore the disapproval of children. They affirm their sexuality. They reject and triumph over loneliness. They open themselves to the psychic surprises — the uncertainties of intimacy. They pursue their happiness.

With new spouses, the remarrieds have the potential to redefine themselves in a profound physical and emotional way. Such is the alchemy that marriage inspires. And so, perhaps, more than any other group of the elderly we've met, they offer the most dramatic examples of old age as a time of discovery and beginning, in which the past is not discarded, but remembered and used in the exciting present and the anticipated future.

Baltimore, Maryland

Malvina and John Brown
Age 71   Age 70

Malvina: I know lots of people over sixty-five who marry; sometimes they marry twenty-five and thirty year-olds. Women have a harder time finding younger men. But I was the lucky one. I'm seventy-one and he's sixty-nine, no, seventy. We've been married since January 20, 1975. I was married three times. This is my fourth marriage. I was nineteen when I married the first time. My husband died when I was twenty-six; I had three children with him.

John: This is my third marriage. When I was about thirty-eight, I married my first wife; that was in 1946; she died in 1970. I was in the Navy for twenty-five years and that kept me on the move. When I came out of the Navy in 1954, I worked for a while at two or three different places. I went to school and took a course in printing. I worked for three and a half years. But the company eventually folded up and moved to Hartford. I retired from printing in December 1966, I think. Then I had a heart attack. I got this house in 1948 while I was still in the Navy. I married my second wife on July 31, 1970, and she died in 1975. It was almost a year before I met my present wife. I don't have any children at all.

Malvina: I was born in New Orleans. I met my first husband in Biloxi, Mississippi. Three months later I came here to Baltimore, and I've been here ever since. My third husband left me a good income. He used to work for American Can Company. I've worked, managing two or three lunchrooms. When I was sixty-two, someone asked why I didn't retire. But I enjoyed work. I'd come home, I'd clean my house, the children would visit on Sunday. When I quit work, that's when I got lonesome. But I wasn't interested in getting married. I didn't go where the men were. I did go to the senior center, though. John and I met square dancing there. It was only my second time at the center. He asked me to be his partner and I said yes; we've been partners ever since.

John: They were forming squares on the dance floor; I saw her and kind of liked her looks. So I went over and asked her to dance, and she got up. I'd been single for only a brief time. A friend had told me to go to the center. I'd watch the dancing sometimes, but then I'd go upstairs to play chess. This time I didn't.

Taking a Chance on Love Again

Malvina: The week after we met, we went to a party at Cross Keys. At the time, I was staying at my son's for a few days. I'd heard about the party, but I didn't want to walk into a dance alone. Then I thought of John all of a sudden. So I got up at 9:00 in the morning, to call him before he went to church. My son heard me, and he said, "Mom, who are you calling?" And I said, "A friend of mine to take me to a dance." "What," he said, "at your age?" "Honey," I said, "go back to bed. You're old-fashioned." We went to the dance. From then on we went steady. We'd go to the movies, or go dancing, or watch television. We saw each other every day at the center, and we'd date every three days or so. I started to care for him. I noticed every little thing about him. How kind, how nice, how clean. He respected me; that was the main thing about him. When some men go with a widow, they start fooling around. He was not that type. He was a gentleman. I wanted a home, somebody to love, somebody to love me, and I know he does.

John: I wanted her to know I didn't smoke or drink. I didn't run around at night time. Sometimes if I was alone at night, I'd take a walk around the block, or I'd do something in the house. I never cared about running around too much. Dance halls, movies, roller skating—the things I liked to do—that all disappeared. I didn't care about going around to bars and cabarets.

Malvina: He always stuck to his wives. That's what the neighbors told me. What a good man he was.

John: I found out she loved life and wanted a lovely life, but she couldn't get it. I saw that deep down in her. I see more of her qualities now I guess than when I first started going with her, because we didn't know each other too well for the short time we were going together.

I wanted to get married again, but I thought I'd just bide my time till I found somebody I liked. I'd dated a couple of times, but nothing meant anything. Malvina was pleasant and looked nice and she chose her words well and she was neatly dressed. She didn't smoke or drink and neither did I. We started going together, and I thought, this is the woman I'm looking for.

Malvina: Then one night he came over to my house. We ate, talked and watched television. When John left at a quarter to twelve, he kissed me for the first time. Right then I knew I could still feel sex and love in my heart for a man.

John: Shortly after that we wanted to go square dancing first thing in the

Malvina and John Brown

morning, so I suggested that she come stay at my place, because I'm closer to the center and she's about one and a half hours away. So she came over and we had dinner and breakfast. Nothing improper. She slept in one bed and I slept in the other.

Malvina: I was a little scared. I was embarrassed. I didn't know if I was doing right or wrong. I wouldn't want my boys to do it. So he said I'd have my own bedroom, and I did. He was such a gentleman all the time, I felt I could trust him.

John: From the first square dance, we liked each other a lot.

Malvina: We had Christmas dinner at my son's. My son had met him the day I'd invited him to that dance at Cross Keys, the second time we saw each other. My son said, "Mom, don't go getting mixed up with a man at your age. Didn't you have enough with three?" I said, "You've got a wife, ain't you? I'm tired of being by myself. He's a nice gentleman and as long as he treats me like a lady, I'm going to keep on going with him." And on Christmas he proposed.

John: We'd talked a few days before about marriage. And we both said we were lonely. Then at her son's, I said, "I don't see why not." And she agreed.

Malvina: This is my first happy marriage. We wake up in the morning with a hug and a kiss. It's wonderful. I'm happier now than I've ever been in my life. And I have three lovely children. I love them, but their father was an alcoholic. I had it rough. My second husband was a manager: he was tight. Then he started being jealous of my sons, and I was very close to my children. He didn't even want me to kiss them anymore.

My third husband was a very good man. A bachelor, never been married, saved his money, had a lovely apartment. I sold my home and moved in with him when we got married. But he had an eighteen-pound tumor I didn't know about; he had high blood pressure, too. He didn't tell me anything. The first thing you know, they called me from American Can and said he had high blood pressure and they were sending him home. I took him to the doctor. He lived for about a year and a half, and then he had a stroke. He left me money. I was so independent when I first met John, I didn't want to get married.

John: My first marriage was very happy. It lasted over twenty years. The second lasted four years. Now I'm happily married again. I can't be any happier.

Taking a Chance on Love Again

Malvina: The happiest day of my life was the day we got married. It was on television nationwide, January 20, 1975. We got married at the center. Three hundred and eighty people came. I had a beautiful gown. All my grandchildren were there. My son gave me away; his wife was the matron of honor.

John: As you get older, friends start drifting away and you get lonely. I was telling Malvina it's nice and warm inside when we're together, and outside, baby, it's cold. Companionship, love, everything that goes along with married life, that's what I was looking for. Get along together, talk together, do things together. I wanted that when I was younger and still do now. This marriage is a little better than the other two. I enjoy it more. We go out a lot and do more things together than I did before. Malvina likes to go dancing; I like to go dancing. My other wife, she didn't like to do things like that. We didn't know people—we didn't go out much. Yes, I'm having more fun now.

Malvina: That's because we have more leisure time, more friends.

John: Yes, the different friends. That means a lot, too. And things have come up with Malvina that never came up before. If she wants to do something, I do it with her; if I want to do something, she does it with me. We share everything together. That's important.

Malvina: That's the same way I feel. We're always together. If he goes to the basement, I'll find two pieces of clothes to wash and I'll be down with him. And when he's finished with what he's doing, he'll wait for me. I don't feel seventy-one years old. I feel about fifty. I feel secure and happy and not lonely. He loves me and I love him. I was afraid because of those other marriages. Until that first kiss. When he gave me that first kiss I knew I wasn't through with love. Sex plays a big part, too. We enjoy it; we just go along slow but sure and easy.

Malvina: I enjoy sex more now. I'm not afraid to get pregnant, and it's exciting. We take our time. And we love and kiss and play around and kid around. It's just different altogether.

John: I guess people who've been married a long time might lose their interest. But we do little romantic things for each other.

Malvina: Everytime we go shopping that man is going to get me something. I have more clothes than I can wear if I live to be ninety. And he has the same taste as I have.

John: Sometimes I pick things out she didn't even know were on the rack.

Malvina and John Brown

Malvina: I love to bake for him and do things that he likes and buy him little things he'd like. Bow ties, something for square dancing, socks or different things I like that I want to see him wear. It just happened to be that we can afford enough.

Malvina: I like to go dancing, I enjoy going out to the store together and eating out. We do that once or twice a week. I haven't found anything wrong with John yet. He seems to be the same man now as before we were married. He helps me up the steps. He does everything that a woman loves a man to do.

John: A woman always likes to hear, "You look nice, you look pretty." I like to get other men to look at her to see what they missed by not marrying her.

Malvina: I always want him to have everything match, so he'll look good. He does the same thing for me. I wouldn't change him for the world. We do a lot of talking about each other. About some of my life, my children. How my second husband did more for my children than he did for me. I've told him a lot about the pain in my past.

John: I feel if you keep a lot of painful things inside, they keep swelling up. Well, I don't have many regrets. A few as far as the service goes. If I had it to do over, I'd do it differently. After I got out of the service, I had things a lot better.

Malvina: I have more bad memories than good ones.

John: I may have bad memories from the service. But I have no regrets about my three wives. I tried to make as good a life as I possibly could for them, and with them.

Malvina: I feel this way; when my time comes, I'll go. But I don't want to go. I'd like to live with John for twenty years. I hate the thought of losing John. I'd rather see me go first. I don't want to leave him, and I don't want him to leave me.

John: I look at it this way. Although I'm in good health now, if God wants me in the next five minutes, that's all right. And if He lets me live a long time, that's all right, too. When you go to bed at night, you say your prayers; you get up in the morning, you thank God for a quiet night's sleep. Live a nice, quiet life, don't worry about death, about dying.

Malvina: I believe in my prayers. God has been wonderful to us.

Tiburon, California

Mary and Fred Taylor
Age 76   Age 72

Fred: I'm seventy-six.

Mary: I'm seventy-two. We've been married seven months.

Fred: I was married for thirty years, separated for several years and then married again for three years. There was a hiatus of two years between my last marriage and my present marriage to Mary.

Mary: My last two marriages were both terminated by death. The first one lasted twelve years, the second one eighteen years, and the third, almost nine years. Both of my last two marriages were wonderful while they lasted. Although those good times ended, I still had to go on. There's always more ahead. During the years I was alone, I had my children around me and was living in a retirement community. I went to classes and took Spanish, French and parapsychology. We had a lot of concerts and other activities and I kept busy. But being alone was no fun.

Fred: I lived a bachelor's life when I was alone, spending much time in Europe. I was involved with my business when I was here, but I often stayed away two or three months at a time. My job and my house on the French Riviera kept me busy, and old friends would come by. Mary and I have known each other for thirty-five years, and I've had my eye on her for the last thirty years, but we were never single at the same time.

Mary: Let's say we've been a mutual admiration society for thirty-five years. We had seen each other occasionally when I was in Italy and he was on the Riviera; however I really didn't think I would remarry. I thought I would just go on being single, but it was lonely.

Fred: My second wife and I had decided to separate on a friendly basis. I was living alone but didn't like it much. This is my happiest marriage. Mary is the woman I've been dreaming about my whole life. She's exactly the girl I wish I had married the first time around.

Mary: I wanted to be loved for what I really was. I was never looking for a man with money or position, but for somebody gentle, loving, sweet and kind. Being good looking and successful didn't hurt, though. None of my other husbands was quite as successful. They were all different though, and satisfied different needs. The first one was a Texas rancher, and I had

Note: Names and places in this interview have been disguised upon request.

Mary and Fred Taylor

my beautiful children with him. The second was a successful banker, musical, handsome and a lot of fun. The third was a poet, a very intellectual person. I learned more while living with him for nine years than I did in college. He was writing a book on Greece when he died. We traveled all over Europe.

So I have grown with each marriage and experience. My education's improved. Now I have a husband who studies astrophysics at the breakfast table and tells me all about it, but we mostly enjoy talking about travel and food. We enjoy each other more than anyone we know. We don't have a chance to get bored. We talk about our families, politics, friends.

Fred: I haven't gotten bored yet. We enjoy reading together and sharing good music. Our friends come by often. We even have a guest cottage. Sometimes we take a picnic lunch and go visiting.

Mary: We have a lovely terrace and we like to have lunch there on the weekends. Usually on Sundays we have a party. I think we're enjoying life in a big way.

Fred: We wake up with laughter and go to bed with laughter.

Mary: People seem very happy that we're married, although some people think we're antisocial because we're so into each other.

Fred: Our two families fit together like a hand in a glove.

Mary: In fact, our grandchildren were best man and maid of honor at our wedding.

Fred: Last May our entire family of fifteen sailed on a 120-foot cruiser to the Greek Islands. Mary arranged the trip.

Mary: I'd wanted my children to share the beauty of Greece with me, so we included all our children and grandchildren. The trip lasted two weeks and they all got along beautifully. We're pretty lucky people.

Fred: You have to go a long way to find anybody luckier than we are, or than I am. Two years ago I was divorced. Mary and I married a year and a half ago. I wasn't feeling well at the end of the second marriage, so I wasn't making plans for myself or thinking of marriage. I was taking it easy, until I saw Mary.

Mary: Fred had a cousin living in Berkeley Hills who was going to Spain and I gave a party for him. He invited a couple of members of his family, and Fred was one of them. My daughter and her husband were there and mentioned a trip we were taking to Honolulu. My son-in-law said to Fred,

Taking a Chance on Love Again

"Why don't you come with us?" He came along, and we saw quite a bit of each other after that, spending almost every weekend together for a year. A year and a half after the trip we got married.

Fred: I courted her with flowers, candy, parties and telephone calls. My telephone bill was four times larger than it is now. I called every night and every morning. Now I can't wait to get up in the morning and take her in my arms and kiss her. Our love life is great. When I was young, I thought old people were sexless, but now I think married love is too good for young people.

Mary: Of course sex is important.

Fred: It's the basis of love. It's part of nature's way of keeping the reproductive process going.

Mary: We don't have to worry about that. The pleasure is as great now as ever; in fact it's even more relaxed, now. And when you're younger you're more jealous. I feel now that I have more security and more sense. People who are jealous for no reason are being stupid. It upsets a lot of marriages. Fortunately, neither of us is possessive, and neither of us would give up our own individuality. I would never allow it to be done to me. I think jealousy has passed for us.

Fred: I wouldn't be jealous because I don't have any fears. At our ages we don't have to worry about anything. We know we're in love and that's it. I've never been more relaxed, as satisfied with life.

Mary: A love like ours can start as a friendship, then become quite deep as it grows. Suddenly something just hits you.

Fred: I didn't discover anything new about her because I had known her for such a long time. She was exactly as I thought she was.

Mary: Nothing has surprised me. I always thought Fred had a great capacity for loving and being loved, but it wasn't fulfilled. I knew I could fulfill it for him and I think I have. I was confident that we would be this happy. We haven't had an argument.

Fred: Never will. I can't see anything that will lead to an argument.

Mary: I can't either. I think we're both mature enough, and we've said to each other, "If there is anything you don't like, tell me." In my first marriage I would just clam up if things went wrong. A lack of communication is bad. We certainly don't lack that — we communicate about everything. We both feel that we get so much more out of being together than the younger people do. We want to be together all the time. We're filled with love and it's very romantic. We've been close and are closer every day, but it's important for our relationship to be involved with other things, too. You grow with every experience. I do yoga, swimming and jogging. I read every morning at the breakfast table.

Fred: I never quit my business, because I would never be satisfied sitting around. The challenge of my business keeps me going. I won't retire until the day I can no longer drive a car.

Two years ago, I had a stroke, but now I'm fine. Both of us have had our arterial systems cleared out, which helps to add a few years. We visit a doctor who gives a series of injections that get all the rust out without having to have an operation. I received the injections and it prevented another stroke. It takes out cholesterol and clears up arthritis. It's very expensive, but it's worth it. Still, if I died tomorrow, I would have gotten a lot more than my share.

We all face death. I would just hate to leave Mary when I'm enjoying her so much. It is selfish to grieve for somebody, because it's your own pain that you're dealing with, not the pain of the departed one.

Mary: I'm not a churchgoer, but I think I'm religious. I believe in God. I believe He's in me. He's not a critical man who's standing over me. He's a great power that's in everything. Still, death is something that you don't want to think about. I have a fear of death because I don't want it to happen right away. When we got married, I said, "If we have a year together, it's worth it to me." We've had seven months and hope to have thirty years. We both think positively about our lives and I think that's why we enjoy it. Whatever we've had has been beautiful.

Colorado Springs, Colorado

Bea and John Morrow
Age 70   Age 69

Bea: We met at the senior citizen center, where we went to play bridge. I was attracted to Mr. Morrow because I thought he was a man of very good character. I liked his lifestyle and the fact that he went to church and was a responsible person. I had a great respect for him. In my lifetime, I hadn't met many like that.

John: It was about three years for me. I really didn't plan on getting married again.

Bea: I definitely didn't. I had a very exciting job for which I traveled around the world, and I wouldn't have given that up for just anyone. I felt very self-sufficient and had a very happy life just as a single person. But I decided to give it up because, well, as far as I was concerned, I found someone I thought would fit into my scheme of living beautifully; we like to do the same things. Even if you become self-sufficient and become able to cope with living alone, it nevertheless is certainly good to have a companion. That is, if you have a happy marriage, and John is so easy to be with. He's an unusual man.

John: I think it's pretty much the same in my case. I just got to the point where I didn't see any reason for not getting married. I felt that I had nothing to sacrifice and everything to gain. I was perhaps giving a lot less than I was getting by getting married. We had a kind of a little thing between us here, because when I had left the East I thought I had given up all this business of tending yards, fixing this and fixing that. I was going to let somebody else do that; but somehow that went by the boards.

Bea: This is the second marriage for both of us. I was sixty-eight.

John: I was sixty-seven.

Bea: I felt that I was going to gain a companion, someone who was stimulating intellectually, someone who was a pleasure to be with. I couldn't see that there was a lot to lose and I still don't see that there was, except that I did sort of look a little over my shoulder. I had been free quite a time, and there are a few attractions, you know, in being free and calling your time your own. But then I thought that what I would have in companionship would more than make that up. And it certainly has.

Bea and John Morrow

I didn't worry about the reaction of my family at all; that was something we talked over ourselves. Perhaps we're rather independent people, because we both have this feeling that we do not want to be a burden to our children. We have worked and planned financially so that we would not be a burden to them. One of the reasons that I kept my job as long as I did was that it took me away from the vicinity where my children lived, and I felt that I was letting them live freer lives. We made this decision to marry completely on our own, and we did not ask them. We just told them and they were all happy, apparently.

John: I don't think they were just interested in our general happiness. I think they were happy to see us get married because I think that maybe they were a little concerned about what would happen to us if we were single. I think they might have felt more obligated to be considerate of our comings and goings, and things like that, if we were single.

Bea: I think there was another factor involved as far as my children were concerned. They thought that I had had the best of life in my experiences. They certainly admired John and respected him, and I think they gave me credit for having enough intelligence not to take this step if it wouldn't make my life happier. I know that when we told them, though they were in a state of shock somewhat, they seemed happy about it.

In fact, I feel now that John's family is just as much mine as my own, and I think he has the same feeling toward my family. It's no longer your children and my children, but our children. It's been beautiful, as far as working out as a family relationship is concerned. As far as other people feeling it wasn't right for us to marry at our age, or society's prejudices about it, we're two individuals who do our own thing. I don't think that we ever had any more fun than the day we had our blood test and the day we went to get our marriage license, because we could see all these people laughing at us, and they couldn't see that underneath it we were laughing just as heartily at their reaction.

John: One of these young nurses came in to take a look to see what a couple of old codgers like us were doing in there getting a blood test. When we went up to the courthouse it kind of gave some of the people up there a chuckle to see us come in for our marriage license. I think we enjoyed that as much as they did. We just had to go through with this. We certainly never considered just living together.

Bea: No. I think we both have certain standards of morality, so that would have not been acceptable to us. Certainly, we would not have done that because we would not have wanted our children to have felt that we would take such a step. We have led fairly circumspect lives, and that just never would be considered.

John: I think one thing we had, as older people getting married, compared to our first marriages, was a lack of misconceptions. We each knew that our mate was human after all, and we didn't hold any big ideas that everything would be just perfect. We learned to just live with it, with another human being.

Bea: I think that we developed a tolerance at this stage of life, and also a set of values that are different from those of younger people. For example, we found a house that we wanted to live in although financially we could have lived in a better one. We are content and very pleased with what we have, whereas with the younger couples there is this striving for so many more material things. We already have it. We're not wealthy, but we're comfortable.

John: I don't know that we have any special problems. I don't know what other people have, but I don't think we have any that a younger couple wouldn't have. I don't think we expect too much from each other.

Bea: I think we give each other enough elbowroom so we can be ourselves. I think that's important. We were told once after we had been interviewed by a college class — one of the students came up and said, "I think your marriage must have been made in heaven." I don't know that we can say that, but we have been very, very fortunate, in that we know each other very, very well, and it has been very comfortable and a happy situation.

I believe that one factor is that we're more tolerant of each other's independence than a younger couple — although we do many things together. Of course since we're both retired, we have many hours together in the home and in our everyday activities that younger people don't have. But at the same time, when John wants to go fishing with the dog, off he goes, and if I want to go to a club meeting, off I go. Then we're happy to be back together after being apart for a few hours. In our marriage, though we haven't been apart for more than a few days, I think we wear well on each other. I believe we've discovered things about each other we hadn't been aware of before we married, but we've been happily married going on two years now.

I don't ever think that we find a boring moment, which I think is quite a great thing in our marriage. Let's take today. John's an early riser, so he usually gets up and the coffee's ready, and then when he hears somebody else stirring, I get a cup of coffee in bed. I don't know how I rate that, but it's great. We read the paper, putter around. We take a look at the garden and see what's happened since yesterday. There are always exciting things happening there. Then breakfast. Then John goes to do some volunteer work at the senior citizen club, and I go out to do some shopping and some odds and ends. We have a lot of errands that I can take care of without his having to go along. Then we'll meet again around 4:30, and we'll come home and have dinner. Then maybe we'll call somebody to come over for the evening, or we may watch TV. We'll find a pleasant way to spend the evening.

John: I think you've said it all; that's pretty much the case. Some of the other times, we'll just pack up and go fishing and spend the day out. We had some relatives visit here. We always keep ourselves busy; so we're not stepping on each other's feet, but we're working side by side.

Bea: I believe that the general public looks upon people of our age as being a little dull mentally, and as not being up with the times. Perhaps we're very fortunate in our group of friends — but we have friends who do exciting things. They have interesting hobbies, and they by no means can be thought of as living in the past. They're living in the present. A little man of eighty-four said to me the other day, "We're not just sitting here waiting our time out, we're making the most of every minute."

It seems to me that a great many senior citizens are finding this a very interesting time of life. As far as John and I are concerned, I think we feel it is one of the best times of life, not discounting anything in the past. At the present, so many of the problems that bothered us at the time — about well, for instance, putting our children through college, the financial problems, the demands that have to be met, and the demands of our job — we're through with them.

A day or two ago, I asked a friend at the center, "What time is it?" He said, "I don't know. I quit watching the clock. Sometimes I don't know what day it is, but I can tell you the month." I think this is a great relief, to get off the treadmill, we do the things that we enjoy doing very much. We always tell these younger people: "Just look forward to these later years." However, there is one big factor here, and that is health. I think one of the reasons that this is such a fulfilling time of life is that we do have fairly good health.

John: We're just going to live until we die. We're going to make the most of it.

Bea: When the experience of death comes, it's going to be another adventure, as many of our experiences have been in the past. We are active in the church, and we have a great faith. We have said to each other, in fact we

Taking a Chance on Love Again

said to each other when we were married, at our age we may not have over a couple of years together. But we decided that those years would be fruitful and more fulfilled together, and we're approaching our second anniversary in better health, in better spirits than we had when we were married. God has been good in giving us these times together. When He calls, we'll go and all will be well.

Worcester, Massachusetts

May and George Brookman
Age 77   Age 73

May: We've been married just one year. I had been married for thirty-eight years when my first husband died. I was widowed for ten years. I have one son.

George: I had been married for fifty-one years minus two months when my first wife died. A year passed between marriages. I have a daughter and a son, four grandsons and a granddaughter.

May: I didn't expect to remarry. I had a very full life and felt that I couldn't cope with watching another man suffer and die. I didn't go out with men, with unmarried women, or to places where I might meet a man.

George: To be frank, when my wife died, I had no thoughts one way or the other about remarriage. My life was quite full, with an interesting job as an industrial engineer. I lived in the outskirts of Atlanta, Georgia, and traveled to various plants. However, I found that I couldn't cook for myself. I lost about twenty-eight pounds and five inches from my middle, which I don't regret because I'm trim now. I had never taken care of a home. I kept it clean, but that was about all. I wasn't lonely, because I was always among people. I was Chairman of the Legislative Affairs Committee of the Worcester Council on the Aging, and I became involved in its nutrition program. I spoke before groups once or twice a week and was coordinator of the National Health Insurance Council in Washington. I spent little time at home.

May: For financial reasons I went back to work after thirty-five years when my husband died. In the ten-year period between marriages, I was fortunate to have a very interesting job in a health organization, since I had experience in that field. I found it very satisfying, and I feel I did a good job. But I became lonely at home. I was a different person the minute I walked out the door at 7:30 A.M., because I knew I had a responsibility, yet when I came home the loneliness started all over again. I rarely accepted invitations of my close friends because I felt depressed and it was unfair to impose this on them.

Six years ago I decided that my job was getting too big and that I couldn't cope with all the responsibility. I decided to move to Worcester because my son lives here. The job salaries here are a disgrace, and I couldn't find a job even though I wanted to work. So I decided to rely on my savings, and I did very well. I rented an apartment, and I furnished it with my things from New York. Almost immediately I began meeting people. My sister encouraged me to join a leisure group which meets once a week. All the members are retired, nice and intelligent. Although I'm not aggressive, I became very active in the group, as has always been my way. I met the Brookmans there and became quite friendly with them. I admired Mr. Brookman right away, praising him wherever I went. He's done a fantastic job for all these people. I had no romantic interests then but accepted my life. I missed companionship and someone to talk to about such matters as world events and editorials in the newspapers. I missed this most — someone to share my thoughts. My advice to anyone in that same position is to go out and meet people. It all worked out for the best. If I had married earlier, I wouldn't have married Mr. Brookman.

George: I definitely do remember the first time May came to the group. It was just forming. I had to evaluate people's fitness as workers or as management material. I immediately recognized that May had specific abilities. I asked her to help me, and we worked together for a couple of years. About six months or so after my wife died, I realized that I was interested in more than a work relationship and I began to see her on a personal rather than just a business basis. I admired and respected this person. I knew that I could care a lot for her as a companion for the rest of my life.

She was very reluctant at first, which I can understand, because I had been a widower for such a short time. In order to spare me embarrassment, she tried to arrange our meetings at places where we wouldn't be seen together in public. I would visit her at her home, or she would come to my apartment, which she had done before. It was nothing new, for the neighbors knew her as a co-worker.

May: I knew that Mr. Brookman had a fine reputation in Worcester, and I didn't want anyone saying anything that would hurt it. After six or eight months I realized that I was being courted. Up until then, I couldn't imagine anything like this happening to me. I was just going through the motions of living, and marriage was not in the cards at all. When Mr. Brookman proposed to me, I was shocked. Gradually I began to accept the idea of remarrying. Now I can't imagine life without marriage. I began to feel there was a new dimension in life, that I was alive again and that I had a definite purpose. It wasn't difficult to begin making meals, as I did years ago. In fact, it was exciting.

May and George Brookman

George: I'm not the kind of man who sits and waits for miracles to happen. Rather, I like to create them. I'm involved in changing the attitude that old people are made of stone, like statues, without feelings. Anyone who thinks that an old person can't do what a young man can is making a big mistake. I felt entitled to love at any age. Age is just a state of mind. When I saw that there was someone I could spend the rest of my life with, I made up my mind to pursue her.

May: When two young people marry, they're very much in love. Then they grow, they raise a family, and they love, but not as they did when first married. I feel I've been twice blessed. I went through the period of respect and companionship and now I'm again experiencing those same feelings of love which I felt over fifty years ago. I never thought that was improper for someone my age at all. It's really a very happy marriage. We sit for an hour at breakfast-time talking. The same thing happens at lunch and dinner. He's a highly intellectual man. He knows something about almost every subject, be it the Bible or American literature. He knows everything! How could I ever be bored?

George: The attitude of our families and friends was beautiful. I had dreaded the reactions of my family, because I'd heard so many stories about children opposing the remarriage of their parents. I realize how very lucky I've been in this respect. My son and my wife's son get along beautifully, like brothers. When I told my daughter about the wedding, she was very glad and happy for me.

May: She was so happy that she called me immediately. My son kissed George with real affection the first time he met him, and my daughter-in-law and granddaughter are crazy about him.

George: May's work exposed her to all types of people. She does what she's interested in, and I do what I like best, which is my writing. We spend more time together than people would at the age of thirty. I can sit down and really discuss things with her. If you had to spend a lot of time with someone who is uninteresting or just a companion, you could become very bored.

May: My marriage to George is new and vibrant. We're very much in love. I don't know how much longer we will live. In our earlier years, we felt we had many, many years ahead; now we feel that in each day we've had a week or a month. This is the way to plan when you are a little older; you make the most out of every minute.

Taking a Chance on Love Again

I don't think that I could remarry just to be able to cook a meal, have a roof over my head, and have someone in the house. I wouldn't have entered into marriage at this time if there hadn't been the physical attraction that we have for each other. We really have a complete life. To us, it's all new and exciting and there were no problems adjusting to each other. I understand that George was never helpful around the house before, but now he helps out with all sorts of tasks. We manage beautifully.

George: The doctor asked me just the other day if sex is still important for me. I told him that my sex life is very satisfactory — just as satisfactory as it was twenty-five years ago. Each woman reacts differently to different things you do, and you adjust. You learn what the other person likes and you act accordingly. The present Mrs. Brookman has a lot of affection and she shows it.

My life has changed in various ways. I've learned how to dry dishes, something I never did before! But seriously, there have been changes. My first wife was a wonderful person with a fine character, but she left most of the important decisions to me. It's rather trying when everything falls on your shoulders. But May naturally expects to be involved in decision-making. It was difficult at first, because I was accustomed to doing everything myself, but now I've learned to discuss and work out any decision, no matter how small. It's a relief. We have independent minds, and we don't always agree, but that is good, too.

My life has changed in other ways. I have been doing much more writing. I was always inclined towards it, but May gives me a lot of support and encouragement. When I first retired at age sixty-eight I was quite frightened and had trouble sleeping, worrying about what I would do next. I don't like to sit and watch TV. When I moved to Worcester I became active in organizations and in the community. Now, with May's support, I write a monthly research article for three newspapers. Currently I'm writing about the *Kaballah* in layman's language, working on a piece about the Dead Sea Scrolls and writing on politics for the local paper.

May: My lifestyle has also changed since my marriage. I used to be invited every day to play mah-jongg at women's houses, but I never accepted, so they don't call me anymore. I sew all my own clothes, bake and still do the volunteer work I've been doing for five or six years.

I've also noted a great change in my decision-making. I really went through a difficult period after my first husband died. For ten years I made my own decisions, so it's very nice to share the responsibility.

George and I also do little romantic things. Today we went to the temple breakfast and heard a lecture. We go to the theater, to museums, to temple on Friday nights, or we spend evenings at home together, just being with one another. I feel that George would do anything for me. He'll work at the typewriter for fifteen or twenty minutes, and then he'll come to me and hug and kiss me. That's romantic. Our life is really very full.

Chicago, Illinois

Madeline and Walter Baer
Age 66   Age 64

Madeline: We've been married for six months.

Walter: I was first married in 1933 and my wife died last year.

Madeline: I had been married for almost forty years when my first husband died three and a half years ago. I have three grown children. Marriage was something that I felt very good about. I had hoped I would remarry, but never dreamed it would really happen.

Walter: Marg, my first wife, had been sick on and off for five years. In the last year of her life, she was very sick. She knew she was terminally ill and we discussed it. She asked me to remarry. I didn't take it too seriously, but she kept saying I should. I told her she would have to let me take care of that. After she died, naturally I was crushed. My kids lived out of town. I had never really thought about remarrying, yet the longer I was alone, the more miserable I became. I had had a very good relationship with Marg. Madeline, Marg and Madeline's husband and I had all been very good friends for a long time. Madeline and Marg went to school together at the University of Wisconsin. Dave and I had been friends even before attending school together on the south side of Chicago. Marg and I went to their wedding, and I was an usher. We lived different kinds of lives but we were always very close, and our kids were good friends, too.

Madeline: When people read this, they may say, "There was probably always something there." Well, there wasn't. We were friends as a foursome but we never thought of each other in a romantic way.

Walter: Over those years our lifestyles were very different, even though we were good friends. Madeline and Dave were very friendly and outgoing people. Marg and I had a close relationship that was more private. We enjoyed each other and enjoyed doing things by ourselves. Our life was centered more around our immediate family and doing things with the family.

Madeline: I came to see Marg almost every day when she was sick. She wanted me to be with her and talk about her illness. She was a very close and important friend, and the loss was a very difficult one for me. Wally was always glad to see me, and I felt his pain a great deal because I had gone through it. My loss had occurred two years before. David had had many heart attacks, and I had suffered and felt for him. Being with Wally was a very easy thing. There was no discussion of whether or not our relationship was right or wrong. Friends of ours would ask us both to dinner and we accepted because it was easy and comfortable.

Walter: I don't know when we realized we were romantically involved. I was feeling more and more comfortable and enjoyed being with her. All of a sudden I realized that I was starting to live again, looking forward to weekends. I went cross-country skiing with my daughter, and then went to dinner at Madeline's. I had to bring my skis with me, and when I brought them into the house, she said, "I would love to go cross-country skiing." The next weekend we went skiing together.

Madeline: I had gone out occasionally with other men before and didn't like anybody I dated. I was resigned to never finding anybody that I would want to live with. I had two close male friends who were married and had been my friends for many years, but I wasn't going to break up a home. One was in his fifties and one was seventy. The others were boring. They were predictable and didn't feel joy in life. Wally has something special. He meets life with excitement and joy and he has a positive attitude about everything he does. I knew something was happening and I was getting involved. I decided to go away for a week.

I wanted to make sure that this was more than escaping from loneliness. I wanted to be positive. I wanted to be with him in every way, and I wanted to make sure that my feelings would be sustained. I needed a sense of commitment, a friend, a marriage to someone who would be my closest friend. I wanted somebody who was my lover physically, who had the maturity I could respect, and with whom I could share things. When I was younger, I didn't really have such clear feelings about my desires. My values were different.

Walter: When she went away, we decided that if she still felt the same way when she came back we would do something about it. We had been discussing it. We decided to get married because we wanted more than just weekends together, and we liked living together. There were no two ways about it for me — we were going to live together married. I wanted the completeness in life that comes in being with another person. Marg and I got married when we were very young, and I lived most of my life as a married person with someone to come home to and someone with whom I shared a commitment. I've found this again, and I consider myself very fortunate.

Taking a Chance on Love Again

Madeline: During the three years I wasn't married, I missed having a friend who cared. I missed cuddling and sharing desperately. I have never felt so good in my life. This marriage is a new opening, a new discovery and a new horizon. You can get involved in clichés, but this is what our marriage really is. It's like a miracle, a very exciting marvelous thing. Every night and every morning is a shared experience. I've matured. We're lucky, too, that we're in good health and that we love life. We're grateful.

Walter: When we decided to get married, we decided we would never say, "One day we're going to do this." We would just do it. We figured that time was not on our side and we had to do what we wanted while we were able. I've had that feeling most of my life. To me, life was to be lived. The enjoyment of life was much more important that its dollar value. Marg and I had some tough years financially because I wasn't producing as much as I could have, but we found the enjoyment of life more important. We weren't frivolous. We traveled as much as we could with the kids, and later we traveled ourselves. It would be a nice day, so we'd go out and have lunch, or we would go up to Wisconsin or stay on the beach for a couple of days.

Madeline: My life was very different. My husband was a merchant and very ambitious. He was in his family's business, and his work took precedence over what he would have liked to have done.

Walter: I'm still working. I'm a supply distributor in a business that I owned. About seven years ago I moved my office to the basement of my home. My customers come here where I work full time. Naturally, I don't think I'll retire. I've got a house here with an acre of property that I enjoy working. As long as I have that and Madeline's satisfied here, I would like to continue. This doesn't interfere with my business, even though I think I spend more than forty hours a week on my property.

Madeline: I love my work. I've been working for twenty years, and I get a great deal of joy from it. When you put your heart and soul in your work, you're bound to be good at it. I reap a lot of psychological benefits from it. And we enjoy the theater, art, walking, biking, skiing, taking trips, exploring.

Walter: We are together a lot. Working at home enables me to have lunch at home. If Madeline's around, we have lunch together. Sometimes we take a walk after lunch. We can't do much more.

Madeline: We do spend a lot of time together. I'm becoming terribly dependent, and I've never been a dependent person. It's a new role for me.

Madeline and Walter Baer

Walter: I think it's important that she not become too dependent. She has always been a very independent, strong person. We may have to look into that. I don't feel more able to cope than before, because there's a great deal of similarity in my feelings now and those in my first marriage.

Madeline: I have a different marriage this time. My first marriage was very happy in terms of having a strong sense of commitment and a feeling of love and being loved, but with a different kind of man. I feel closer to Wally because we have time to ourselves. David was busy. Some of it is a function of my age. Over the years I've sorted out those things that are meaningful to me. During this last part of my life, I know what I want to do. I don't want to waste my time, as before. Because David didn't have time, I created activities for myself. I don't want to do that anymore because now I want to spend my time with Wally. Not having the children gives us more time to spend together.

Walter: I think it's easier adjusting to another person, now. Small things become unimportant. Living together with a mutual commitment becomes important. Our lifestyle is different. Madeline is certainly not the same as Marg was, but the difference is very incidental and very inconsequential in terms of the major things. Our meals are different, but they're fun. Marg was a gourmet cook, and Madeline really doesn't care. There's a great similarity in their warmth, honesty, straightforwardness and feeling of trust they give me. Yet they differ in a number of ways, and I enjoy that. There's a fundamental decency about both of them which is important.

Madeline: When I was going out with those men for three years, I realized that a man had to have the integrity of commitment. David had it and Wally has, but I don't see it in a lot of people, even some of my close friends. A sense of humor is another common denominator we share. That's basic.

Walter: What I find special about Madeline is her wonderful zest for life. Now I meet more people and enjoy it, different kinds of people in a different milieu. I think Madeline has exposed me to a lot more culture than I had before. Life is different.

Madeline: There were jumps to get over. Wally's daughter was very close to her mother, and I think she was disturbed that he remarried so soon after her mother's death. I was sensitive to her feelings, but I made up my mind that our marriage was going to work.

Walter: I had a long talk with my daughter. Madeline and I made no bones about what was going on. We were very honest and frank about everything. My daughter was delighted about my new life, but she, understandably, felt that there was someone in her mother's place. Madeline handled it so beautifully and so well by explaining that she had gone through the same thing. Her father had been widowed and remarried and she could identify with Betsy's feelings. I think she did a far better job with my daughter than I did with hers.

Madeline: My daughter was delighted and happy for me, but I think there was some natural resentment. What was it going to do to our relationship? Her brothers, too, wondered about this. I learned that they all talked to each other about this. She even called a friend of mine who's a psychologist to ask if my behavior were normal. I hadn't been talking to them on the phone as I had before. They were so worried because I sounded so different on the telephone. They could always tell when Wally was in the room.

My daughter and her family came to visit us, and we all went on a trip together. She and Wally had quite a heated discussion. Wally showed great anger, the only time I've ever seen him angry in relation to us. She was very upset, and it was the first time I had seen her cry in years. It was very difficult for both of them, because they are both very strongminded. She went home and there was some correspondence.

Walter: She was upset because her mother seemed different. She intimated that I was changing Madeline and trying to take her away from her daughter. I didn't handle the situation as well as I should have. After they left, I wrote a letter apologizing, hoping that by our next meeting we could be better friends. We haven't gotten together yet. I got a letter back in which she said that her son asks for me. I'm trying to make the relationship light and humorous, if possible.

Madeline: We're going out to visit her for Christmas. Wally thought it might be a good idea if I went out a little earlier and spent some time alone with her. She was very responsive to that idea. I haven't been alone with her since I've been married. I don't feel I've lost the intimacy I had with my children. The closeness is still there. I feel exactly the same way about them now as I did before I married.

Walter: We do romantic things for each other. We enjoy little corny things. When she goes out and comes back and has a little something for me, it melts me.

Madeline: Wally brings us our breakfast in bed every day. Breakfast time is our special hour together. We read the paper, talk, discuss everything we have to do. I got flowers on our six-month anniversary. I love his touching me, holding my hand when we walk down the street. We also have a double bed, which I never had before in my life.

Walter: Sex is just as important to me now as when I was younger. I found that in the early days of our relationship I had some difficulty in performing. Madeline was very tolerant and understanding and we were able to laugh and joke about it until it became satisfying.

Madeline: Tremendously so. I think it's a very important part of our relationship. It gives us both great pleasure. It's very loving, very exciting and very satisfying.

Walter: I don't think our satisfaction has anything to do with the newness of someone else after so many years with one person. I don't find any strangeness because it developed gradually.

Madeline: It's almost like it was waiting. It's different. It's very ongoing and even amazing, because there's a potency you would expect to find in very young people. Sexual desire, craving and satisfaction are there. My first husband had been in and out of the hospital with heart trouble so there had to be less of a sexual relationship. There was great restraint and fear with Dave because of his serious heart trouble. Sex with Wally is very satisfying.

Walter: Death is the end of life, and I regret my life ending. I know and accept it must end. Any immortality that I will have will come through my children, just as I came from my mother, father, grandmother. I have no other views, although in the back of my mind I hope there's something more than just plain existence. I don't know what goes on out there in space. Maybe there's another world out there to which we're going. I just can't conceive that in all the time before now and all the time there will be, I won't be part of it.

Madeline: I used to have a strong fear of dying, but with maturation came more of a settling influence. I had lost a parent and had a great fear of losing someone or of having to leave, because so much had to be done. That upset me terribly. Now I feel differently. I have a much more tranquil feeling about death. I have a feeling of becoming part of the natural process and the elements. My feelings of immortality are about nature and knowing that everything goes on. In those feelings I receive consolation. Wally said your children and grandchildren carry on, and that continuum is my concept of a natural flow of life. That doesn't mean I won't get depressed

Taking a Chance on Love Again

about having to face any loss or illness of my own. During difficult times, when I've had to try very hard, I've known that there's something that makes it worthwhile. This time with Wally is one of the highlights of my life. There isn't any time of the day that I'm not aware of it and terribly grateful for it. It's so wonderful.